"Yantzi draws on current theories of counseling offenders, restorative justice philosophy, Christian theology, and over twenty years of experience. He offers compelling alternatives to address complex issues for the church and community in responding to sex offenders."
— *Caroline Duimering, Social Worker*

"Police officers experience many sources of social and emotional pain in their work as keepers of the peace. That stemming from sexual abuse ranks among the greatest and, until recently, most intractable. On the other hand, police services everywhere are discovering the healing potential of restorative justice principles. Applying those principles to the damage of sexual abuse, as Yantzi does here, gives us great hope that the pains of this particular offense need not be sustained forever."
— *Rob Davis, Senior Constable, Waterloo Re~*

"Yantzi's book sets out some ~f   ~om the struggles of the 80s an   and to forge useful responses   ers of the new century will ex,   ..uch pioneers like Yantzi have la~
— *Dave Worth, Executive .   ..~onite Central*
    Committee Ontario

"All humans are made in the image of God, even sexual offenders. Most of us have to break through many stereotypes, fears, and hurts to see an offender's humanity. We also need to set appropriate boundaries for everyone. Mark Yantzi works through dignity and boundary setting, so churches can be communities of restoration for everyone. Recommended for pastors, elders, and church leaders."
— *Brice Balmer, Addictions Counselor, Pastor*

"The relationship aspect of child sexual abuse is the place in which much of the damage is rooted. It is critically important to include this in the healing process. Sexual abuse survivors and those who offend sexually are human beings who become connected to each other, and fragmented within themselves, by unspeakable behavior of a sexual nature.

"In a respectful and sensitive manner, Yantzi uses his understanding of sexual offending, his groundbreaking work with facilitated dialogue, and his compelling arguments to apply restorative justice to sexual abuse issues. He opens the door and shows us the way back to the realm in which incest and child sexual abuse occur—the realm of relationship.

"One act of sexual abuse affects many people in complex ways often difficult to see and understand. If there is no dialogue, transformation, or reconciliation between victim and offender, shame and secrecy can dominate their lives and relationships, and often affect the lives and relationships of those around them who 'know' but do not speak.

"*Sexual Offending and Restoration* redirects our attention to the victims, offenders, families, and communities who've 'lived it,' and who 'live with it.' Honoring time, process, and people, Yantzi takes away an important taboo against speaking about sexual abuse. He does this by bringing together everyone affected by sexual crimes, instilling courage in them, and providing tools for them to restore what was lost, to overcome losses, and to reclaim lives that have purpose, control, dignity, and hope.

"Restoring victims, offenders, and their relationships creates a foundation for healing and justice that will extend to families and the culture. This will serve the needs of victims and communities better than punishment alone, or merely suppressing offending behaviors."

— *Deborah Ingraham, Activist for Restorative Justice,*
  Former Incest Survivor Litigant

SEXUAL
OFFENDING
A N D
RESTORATION

Mark Yantzi

Herald
Press

HERALD PRESS
Waterloo, Ontario
Scottdale, Pennsylvania

Canadian Cataloguing-in-Publication Data
Yantzi, Mark, 1946-
   Sexual offending and restoration
Includes bibliographical references
ISBN 0-8361-9081-5
1. Sex offenders—Rehabilitation. 2. Sexual abuse victims—
Counseling of. I. Title.
HQ71.Y36 1998   364.15'36   C98-931839-7

The paper used in this publication is recycled and meets the mini-
mum requirements of American National Standard for Information
Sciences—Permanence of Paper for Printed Library Materials, ANSI
Z39.48-1984.

Bible quotations are from the *New Revised Standard Version Bible,*
copyright 1989, by the Division of Christian Education of the
National Council of the Churches of Christ in the USA.

To Henry Yantzi, my father and friend,
who died on July 12, 1995,
as I began writing this book.
His life and ministry modeled
acceptance of all people
and genuine caring,
whatever their situations or past actions.

Contents

Foreword

Yantzi espouses honesty and openness as key elements in the healing process. He deals skillfully with our tendency toward secrecy in the family and Christian community, noting that such secrecy takes power away from the victim.

The author's insistence on honesty also has the offender's best interest in mind. Without honesty, "the offense seems less serious than it really is," he points out. The offender is not required to face the agony he has caused so many people.

Yantzi effectively uses the insights of a Book Reference Group to validate and substantiate the real people behind the labels for victims-survivors and those who sexually offended.

He develops a compelling case for changing the generational patterns of secrecy, denial, and shame-based silence which have surrounded the topic of sexual abuse. Yantzi calls us to replace those patterns with a biblically based model of honesty, discipline, healing, and restoration.

How we wish we could have given this book as a resource to a woman who approached us one day after a class. It might have helped her work through her pain and bondage to a place of peace and freedom. We had just concluded a series on forgiveness and had encouraged our class not to seek revenge against those who had hurt them, but to let God "avenge," according to Romans 12:19.

The woman approached us. Her honest question revealed her deep hurt: "What do you do when you don't believe God will adequately avenge the wrongdoer?"

She was referring to a man of the cloth who had sexually abused her over thirty years ago, when she was six years old. Her greatest fear was that her offender would repent, turn to Christ, and spend eternity in heaven rather than suffering in hell for the pain he had caused her.

This true story illustrates some of the devastating effects of sexual abuse. First, the personal sexual violation of a little girl. Second, abuse of power by one in authority. Third, refusal to confront the abuse for fear of resulting social turmoil. Fourth, disregard for the human soul of the offender. Fifth, the silence of the Christian community. Sixth, lack of a procedure to bring healing, discipline, and restoration for those involved.

With honesty, justice, compassion, and love, Mark Yantzi deals with these issues in *Sexual Offending and Restoration*. His proposal for restorative justice shows Christian concern for all those involved in abusive relationships.

We are thankful that this resource is now available, and we will use it extensively in ministry. It brings a much-needed word of hope to a population marked by despair.

— *Paul and Virginia Friesen, Coauthors,* Restoring the Fallen: A Team Approach to Caring, Confronting and Reconciling

— *Virginia Friesen, Conference Speaker*

— *Paul Friesen, Family and Men's Ministries,*
  Grace Chapel, Lexington, Massachusetts;
  Family Ministries, Gordon-Conwell Theological Seminary

Preface

I have written this book to provide a resource for people who are addressing the issue of sexual abuse, whether personally, in their family or extended family, or in the broader church and community. By using a restorative justice[1] framework and with extensive help from survivors of sexual abuse and those who have offended, I outline the scope of abuse and its destructive impact. I draw on the courageous stories of many individuals. Thus I point to new paths of healing from sexual abuse, and new ways of restoring wholeness to individuals and caring communities.

As indicated in chapter 1, major inspiration has come from men and women recounting their stories of sexual abuse. I begin my acknowledgment and thanks by recognizing their contributions and their permissions to use their accounts and reflections. Without their efforts, this book would not have been possible. Because of the nature of their sharing, in many cases they are identified only by the pseudonyms that they chose. However, they are aware that their brave examples provide models for others to open up the dreaded secret of sexual abuse. Their personal statements are in appendix 1.

Various people read and gave comments on the first draft of the text. Their thoughtful and probing comments and evaluation of the first draft gave me great help in improving the book. This group included Brice Balmer, Heather Block, Caroline Duimering, Esther Epp-Tiessen, Carolyn Holderread

Heggen, Gordon Husk, Mary Martin, Tina Mast Burnett, Sharon McCallum, Charles Taylor, Dave Worth, Eunice Yantzi, and Howard Zehr. Thank you!

Melissa Miller provided invaluable support with editing and clarifying the content. Because of her own knowledge and writing in this field (see bibliography), she was a consistent source of information, clarification, and encouragement. She believed in the importance of this writing project at times when I doubted.

Mennonite Central Committee Ontario provided financial assistance to make it possible for me to write this book. This demonstrates an ongoing commitment by an agency to find creative new ways to deal with complex social issues. I appreciate their support.

Community Justice Initiatives helped in various ways. The agency provided space for the more than twenty meetings of the Book Reference Group and various other groups. The staff from the Community Mediation Services and Victim-Offender Reconciliation Program were understanding and supportive. Mary Dendekker, Caroline Duimering, and Jennifer Weicker, my co-workers in the Sexual Abuse Treatment Program, were helpful in so many ways. They carried some of my duties because of my work on the book.

The regular breakfast club with Dave Worth and Brice Balmer offered a place for me to debrief about the book and other aspects of my life. Similarly, the members of my house church were ready with support and encouragement as the process unfolded.

Finally, I want to thank my family. Our sons, Jamie and Michael, were always encouraging. Special thanks to my wife, Glennis, who endured the hours I spent at the computer and understood those countless times when I was not physically at the computer, but my mind still was!

—*Mark Yantzi*
  Kitchener, Ontario

1

Opening Our Eyes and Starting to Talk

I had concluded a Sunday morning message on sexual abuse, with a focus on those who offend. I stood at the back of the church and greeted the worshipers as they filed out of the sanctuary. One man shook my hand and commented, "It's a good work you're doing!" I was struck not so much by his comment as by his tone and body posture, the distance he kept between us while shaking my hand. He seemed reluctant to get too close, as though there was a danger of contamination coming through me, from the persons I work with every day.

For me, that incident has become symbolic of the pervasive wish we have as a society to avoid facing and handling something as repugnant as sexual abuse, particularly abuse of children. I understand such a reaction. I believe it is important to realize that much of our inability to face this painful issue can be traced to our deep-seated uncertainty. Often we don't know about sexual abuse because we don't ask, and we don't ask because we really don't want to know. This head-in-the-sand approach perpetuates the tragedy of child sexual abuse.

A Resource in Dealing with Sexual Abuse

As you read this book, I will take you directly and sometimes painfully into a consideration of the complex issues of sexual abuse. You will hear the perspectives of various persons affected by sexual abuse. The focus is on those who have offended. However, to handle this issue wholistically, we must be fully aware of the gravity of the hurts of the victim-survivors.

This approach is helpful when working with persons who have offended, whose own life stories are quite painful. It is important to respond to their pain with empathy. I balance my empathetic approach to their pain with an awareness of how their abusive actions have harmed others. This balancing is essential to provide a productive framework for constructive change and growth.

How Language Is Used

I prefer to use the phrase "a person who has sexually offended" rather than "sex offender." The longer term avoids destructive labeling and provides an incentive and expectation that there will be changed behavior. However, this does not mean that I minimize abusive behavior or its effects. Individuals may refer to themselves as "sex offenders" or "offenders,"and I sometimes will use the same terms since they are less cumbersome. Yet in some situations, I use the more verbose "person who offends" or "person who has offended" to underscore the importance of separating the person from their behavior.

For many who have been victimized by sexual abuse, the term "survivor" represents their growth and change from being simply a "victim," which might be taken as a passive and backward-looking term. Since this is their self-chosen term of overcoming, I will often use it. "Survivor" or "victim-survivor" is not a limiting label but a term affirming the resilience of the human spirit in overcoming deep hurts.

Much of the material in this book comes from cases of child sexual abuse. We will also consider the sexual abuse of adult women and men, and the situation arising when church leaders have abused children and adults.

In my work with sexual abuse, most of the survivors have been female, and most of those offending have been male. This is consistent with findings elsewhere.[1] Later in the book, we will consider gender factors. The gender dynamics of female victims and males who offend are consistent with the power dynamics in our society that contribute to abuse. There is a growing awareness that a significant number of adult men have been sexually abused as children; in my work I am seeing an increase in the number of male survivors. Growing anecdotal and research findings show that women who offend are more prevalent than was earlier thought.[2]

To respect the variety of situations in which abuse occurs, I will generally use the term "person" rather than "he" or "she."

The term "sexual abuse" refers to a sexual act of aggression that involves misusing power and violating the trust of a vulnerable person. To many, "aggression" indicates a physically violent act. However, sexual violence is not always openly aggressive. The root of *violence* is *to violate*, and sexual abuse is a violation. We will consider this further in chapter 2.

The Process of Writing This Book

After developing a draft outline for this book, I invited eight people, four women and four men, to form a group. Each had some direct personal experience or involvement in sexual abuse issues. A student in counselor training also joined the group and helped to facilitate the process.

Together we developed guidelines to follow as we discussed the thirteen chapters. We agreed that the focus of the group was to contribute information and experiences for the book. We concurred that we were not creating a therapy group, though we hoped that group involvement would be therapeutic for participants. We agreed on rules for confidentiality and for what we expected of each member. Participation would be voluntary. We also agreed to make decisions by consensus and to be respectful of each other.

The focus for the group was not on the participants as individuals but on the members' experiences as a backdrop for developing a tool to assist others' healing. We believed that in the process of helping others, individuals would experience personal benefits as well.

At the outset I did not know whether it would be positive

and helpful to bring together those who had offended and those who were abused. Though I believed strongly that such perspectives should form the foundation of this book, I did not know how the participants would find the group experience. I am happy to report that it was quite helpful. The group provided me with useful material for this book. There was also a level of cooperation that I did not anticipate.

This task brought together people with divergent experiences that could have led to confrontation, defensiveness, or hostility. The individuals, well aware of the harm done by those who had offended, were able to engage in an inclusive process; everyone offered their insights for the common task.

The difference in focus may seem minor, but it became significant. In this setting everyone could contribute equally. We acknowledged the pain of each one. Everyone agreed that the abusive acts were wrong. This set the groundwork for truly creative dialogue; I have sprinkled the results throughout the book.

Appendix 1 gives a summary personal statement from each of the participants in this *Book Reference Group,* using their assumed names: *Alexandra, Chip, Gary, Iris, Jimmy, Rebecca, Rob, Samantha,* and *Steve.* The reader will quickly become familiar with these names.

I admire and respect these pioneers in this venture. Many of the quotations in the following chapters come from their sharing. They have helped to deepen and expand my understanding of the impact of sexual abuse and differing responses to it. A vertical bar alongside marks comments by them and others, based on their direct experience and journey toward healing.

The Rest of the Book

The following chapters will lead readers to explore new avenues of response to sexual abuse. While abuse has been with us throughout recorded history, only recently have we begun to name it, heal from it, and develop means of preventing it. I believe we make a vital *preventive* step by working with, learning from, and listening to the perspectives of those who have offended.

Chapter 2 considers the effects of sexual abuse. The confusing and disorienting acts of sexual abuse take their toll on all. We will consider the dynamics of power, violence, and relationship.

In chapter 3, we explore why sexual abuse takes place; why it was a part of our past, from biblical times and before; why it continues today; and why we will need to continue to cope with it in the future. The church, which seeks to support families, faces a difficult task when a sexual boundary violation occurs in a family and threatens the survival of the family unit. In the past, the church has supported the family unit's survival at the expense of the safety and well-being of persons harmed by the abuse. Now the church is challenged to protect victims from further harm.

The focus for chapter 4 is restorative justice that seeks to deal with the hurts, using healing creative responses. Today there is a strong concern about crime and violence, but punitive ways of responding to crime are not achieving the desired ends. In this restorative framework, the rights of victims, offenders, and others affected are respected and protected. The principles of a restorative justice model include respect, integration, democracy, advocacy, and honesty.[3]

In chapter 5, principles outlined in chapter 4 are applied to a case example. How can we bring restorative justice to a family where sexual abuse has occurred? How do the principles apply? What are the results?

Chapter 6 uses a case example to outline the devastation of clergy abuse, a church leader sexualizing a relationship with a child or adult. We will explore the challenges of facing the abuse by considering all persons affected by such acts, including the broader church body. This chapter will provide information on the impact of the abuse on church life and will suggest procedures for handling such issues.

In chapter 7 we consider various people's perspectives on their hurts and the avenues they have found that bring healing and recovery. The journeys will vary for women or men, for those who were victimized, for those who offended, and for people who are close family or friends to either group. *An underlying conviction is that all persons share a journey toward healing.* We want to respect the reality of those journeys, recognizing similar patterns without attempting to blend them into one.

Chapter 8 continues this theme. It seeks common ground in human experience by exploring unresolved past hurts. When we can come to terms with the experiences and hurts we all have, we can build bridges of understanding to others who were harmed or to those who have harmed others. Only then will we be able to walk with those in the church community who experience the pain of sexual abuse.

Chapter 9 asks what forgiveness means and how it applies. Why is this question so often directed to persons who have been victimized rather than to those who have offended? How can we avoid having it become a "should" for persons already struggling to cope with the aftermath of their trauma? How do Christians integrate their beliefs about forgiveness with the deep wounds of sexual abuse?

Chapter 10 looks at how a caring church works with those in the community who have sexually offended. In the past, people used denial or silence to deal with such issues. Given this legacy, churches find it a challenge to be sensitive to all the parts of the community—survivors, those who have offended, and family members and friends. It is difficult to find a balance between respecting the confidentiality and privacy rights of persons affected and making the church a place of healing for all. Case examples will show that efforts have not always been successful, yet there are glimmers of hope and optimism.

A survivor of sexual abuse may choose to confront the person or persons who sexually abused him or her and may ask one or more individuals to facilitate dialogue. Chapter 11 provides first-person accounts from individuals who have participated in such a process. Procedures are outlined to help make this a healing experience. Some will not choose this route, and it would not be useful for every individual.

Chapter 12 faces some hard questions and includes an

example of a difficult case that was handled openly and coura-geously. We will consider other examples of challenging situa-tions and explore the limitations of the restorative justice model.

Chapter 13 looks to the future. By further application of the outlined principles, we consider additional examples of how we might confront sexual abuse. These include a neighborhood meeting with an individual recently released from prison, a sex-ual abuse prevention workshop planned by those most affected, and a series of dialogues between a survivor and a person who offended.

Chapter 14 offers the observations of a family who dealt with sexual abuse. Eight years later they reviewed the experi-ence, noting the ways that they were still coping with the abuse. Finally, the epilogue looks at broader issues which need to be addressed to prevent the cycle of abuse from happening.

Why I Work with Those Who Have Offended Sexually

It is not pleasant to read about the things discussed in these chapters. Some of the language is explicit and direct. As in my opening story, I understand that many find it difficult to do any-thing about the needs and issues of those who offend sexually. I am always encouraged by the many volunteers, both men and women, who have worked and continue to work on sexual abuse issues. They too have faced hard questions:

"You're volunteering to do *what?*" The disbelief in her friend's voice was overpowering.

In a more tentative tone, she repeated, "I'm volunteering to co-facilitate a group for sex offenders."

"I can't image why you would want to work with those per-verts," he declared. "I can't believe you, putting yourself into such a situation. You're not only a bloody bleeding heart, you're also a stupid one!"

Volunteers who co-lead groups for men who have offended sexually often describe similar reactions from their friends and acquaintances. Given the strong public reaction to persons who sexually abuse others, particularly children, it is important to consider why we must meet the challenge of working with those who have offended. Here are some of my reasons:

1. Preventive work begins by looking at the whole system surrounding the sexual abuse of children.

From talking with survivors and offenders, we have gathered evidence that sexual abuse patterns do not usually end with a single generation. Instead, they typically occur through generations in families, sometimes skipping a generation, but eventually recurring. By focusing on the nature of abuse as a system, we can learn how to stop it.

It is essential to provide therapeutic support for those who have been harmed physically, emotionally, and spiritually by the devastation of child sexual abuse. However, if we consider only the victim's needs, our work is incomplete. That is like mopping up the mess from a dripping tap without fixing the leak. It is shortsighted and reactive to concentrate on the *effects* while ignoring the *causes*. Dealing only with effects does not move us toward an abuse-free society.

2. I believe that people can change, including individuals who have offended sexually.

There is a pervasive belief that persons who have offended once cannot change and will repeatedly offend.[4] Frequent media accounts of repeat "child molesters" or "pedophiles" create an atmosphere of despair, thus undermining a hopeful, restorative approach to the issues.

This is difficult to deal with because all offenses are unacceptable; repeat offenses are even more repugnant and create a sense of hopelessness for the individual and the community. The hopeful news is that not everyone who has offended does reoffend!

There are persons who fit the stereotype of a repeat offender. Measures need to be taken to restrict their activities. Members of their communities need to be informed of their release from prison. To avoid more offenses, communities need to take appropriate precautions (see chapter 13, case 1).

Even as I believe that people can change, I believe we must be aware of the need for restrictions and safeguards. It is necessary to provide additional long-term external constraints while internal controls are being developed by the person who has offended. That person's family and friends need to be educated to think about long-term solutions to an extremely difficult problem. They need to avoid giving in to the wish for a "quick fix," for "everything to be back to normal right away."

3. I have been encouraged by the many men who demonstrate sincerity and deep commitment to make fundamental changes in their lives.

I have been affirmed in my belief that people can change. I have met men and women who have offended sexually and yet are facing their issues and previous irresponsibility in a responsible manner. Such actions give me hope that committed people can eventually disentangle the multilayered problem of sexual abuse.

I am impressed by the number of individuals who can experience significant and sustainable change if we give them a supportive environment that respects them as people in spite of their past actions. To change, they need facilitators alongside them, helpers who firmly challenge their faulty and deeply ingrained belief systems, and resolutely confront their previous views of their abusive behaviors.

When persons grapple with their experiences that drive their out-of-control existence, they recognize how freeing it is to face their demons. In a group setting, individuals have the opportunity to form supportive mutual relationships with others who have had similar experiences and problems. When this happens, seeds for renewal are sown.

Sadly, I also live with the gnawing awareness that some individuals will disappoint me and hurt someone else. While I am troubled by this awareness, I choose not to be defeated. Instead, it drives me to increase my efforts to do better work.

4. I have been heartened by the efforts of women and men who are survivors of sexual violation.

Those who have experienced sexual abuse have every reason to be skeptical about the sincerity of those who are involved in the offender program. I value their queries and find their perspectives helpful. My co-workers and I can easily become so focused on the pain of the offender that we lose the perspectives of those affected by the abuse. The effects of sexual abuse are not superficial or short-term; survivors struggle with the devastation for many years.

Along with healthy skepticism from survivors, I have received encouraging response from various women and men who are survivors of sexual abuse. They say it gives them hope that things can change. They tell me that it is valuable for them to interact either directly or indirectly with those who have offended. Often their own perpetrator is still denying that anything improper happened. The survivor's isolation is increased if family members do not believe their experiences.

I am encouraged when survivors tell me their healing is aided by knowing there are persons who acknowledge sexual abuse of children and other powerless people. Such efforts affirm the validity of their experiences and assist them in their struggle to overcome the pervasive cloud of sexual abuse.

5. Work with men who have sexually offended challenges the tenets of my commitment to restorative justice.

I believe strongly in the importance of bringing healing to broken relationships. Applying this belief to sexual abuse issues is probably as challenging a proposition as any I can imagine. I wrestle with a seemingly endless set of philosophical, practical, ethical, and moral issues.

I do not wish to put a surface bandage on a gaping wound to make it appear better than it is. In addition, I feel that we cannot have full restoration in all situations. I also know that when there is a restorative option, individuals sometimes pressure a victim, directly or indirectly, to "reconcile" for the sake of the family, for the Christian community, or for whatever the reason may be. These pressure moves are not constructive or healing, and they do not fit with restorative justice as I understand it.

It is important to keep searching for new ways to deal with issues surrounding childhood sexual abuse. This horror has been allowed to continue for too long. I want to explore openly other ways of tackling this old issue. I recognize that I am opening myself up to criticism and challenge from others regarding my interventions. At the same time, I hope that others, whether victim-survivors, offenders, or other community members, will share and dialogue with me and with others working in this field as we seek to learn and grow together.

Conclusion

The process of writing this book has been enriching for me. I have found myself looking less to textbooks for answers to many questions. Instead, I have received more satisfying and complete answers from people with personal knowledge and experience. They point me to widely divergent alternate paths for healing.

I invite the reader to continue this dialogue. Interact with what is written here. Test it with persons you know for their perspectives. I am sure that in the conversations you will find an avenue for deepening relationships.

Ultimately, relationships are the vital links that restore our sense of being connected to the world around us and enable us to find our own healing paths. As we nurture our relationships, we will find the healing we all need.

2

The Hurts
of Sexual Abuse

"**W**hat do you mean when you talk about sexual abuse?" people often ask me when I make presentations. Generally I hear an edge in the questioner's tone. I know that she or he is struggling to understand and to come to terms with a subject that for centuries has been shrouded in denial and secrecy. As a society, we are finally removing the shrouds from this painful reality. It is often a confusing task.

Definitions are important. We began that process in chapter 1 and now need to expand our understanding of this issue. First, we will consider common responses to sexual abuse discussions, responses that block healing and add to the hurt. Then we will ponder the impact of sexual abuse from the perspectives of those who have been affected by it or have contributed to harming others. The headings of *physical, sexual, emotional,* and *spiritual* will frame the discussion.

Whatever categories we use, we are talking about great pain that is difficult to measure and describe. One member of the Book Reference Group explains:

> *Rebecca:* Viktor Frankl, who lived in Nazi concentration camps for years, said that pain is like a gaseous substance inside a container. No matter how much pain there is, it fills the container.[1]

Common Responses

Rebecca: "Wouldn't being shot by a gun be as bad or worse than being sexually abused?" people ask me. The answer to that question is no, it wouldn't be worse. If someone had shot me when I was a child, I would have been rushed to the hospital and received care. People would not have expected me to keep it a secret, and most of all, they would have believed me.

The wound would leave physical evidence; I could point to the scar. Finally, if I died as a result of my injury, I wouldn't be around to feel the shame, guilt, self-blame, and worthlessness that result from sexual abuse.

In my family, there are many tragedies we can discuss, but sexual abuse is not one of them. Physical suffering is a badge of honor and a regular topic of discussion. Even divorce is an acceptable subject. The community relays such news by praying for Harry's cancer or the Browns' marriage.

Your family may have a different list of acceptable topics, but I imagine you share with Rebecca's family the taboo about incest:

Rebecca: Incest cannot be discussed; it's not safe to pray about it. What are we saying by our silence? That God is somehow not aware that the abuse happened? That God cannot handle it? That we are without hope, without help?

Because there is so much shame and secrecy about sexual abuse, people often do not believe the victim and actually blame the victim for opening up a painful topic. That usually doesn't happen when someone has suffered a physical injury.

To measure the seriousness of something, we often compare it to similar events. Because we perceive physical suffering as more serious and more observable and graphic, we seem to rate psychological pain, such as from sexual abuse, as less serious and more under the control of the sufferer. "Why can't she just get over it?" we ask.

At a social event, I overheard two snippets of conversations.

The first concerned a car accident. "Was it serious?" one person inquired.

"No," came the reply, "just a few banged-up fenders. They were really lucky!"

In the same room, I overheard another conversation about a man who had recently disclosed that he had been sexually abused as a child. Again came the question, "Was it serious?"

The response was startling: "No, just touching."

In my work, I've found that men who have offended sexually use a similar gradation of "seriousness." The men may even name their offenses and then assert, "I never forced her to do anything she didn't want to do." Thus they imply complicity, equality, and shared responsibility. But nothing is further from the truth.

I have frequently found it difficult to discuss this issue with men who have offended sexually. On one level, they acknowledge their sexual abuse of a child, but they are often quick to point out that it was "just touching" and there was no "violence." I usually reply that what happened was a sexual *violation*, substituting a root word for violence.

Whether the victim is a child or an adult, the "defense" often offered by the accused is that there was no physical force used. The accuracy of that statement should be explored further. Even where there was no *physical violence*, there was a *violation*. The adult who violated must take full responsibility.

Steve, a member of the Book Reference Group, comments on his difficulty in coming to terms with what he had done in offending against his daughter:

> *Steve:* The thing that I struggle with is that I was "laid back" with my daughter. I was very cunning in how I achieved what I wanted to get. I had difficulty coming to terms with what I did as a violent act. At that time I felt so powerless. Everything around me was out of control; I hated my job, and there were things in the family that were out of control. I felt really powerless within that, but when I was abusing, I felt a sense of power and control.

These are situations where persons use their *relationship* with someone who is vulnerable. They abuse the trust persons tend to have in people they know.

This is less applicable in situations of rape or sexual assault where the aggressor is a stranger. However, even in situations of acquaintance rape or date rape where aggressive force may have been used in the assault, those who offend often say that the person victimized was responsible or cooperated. It is easy to see how such situations are misunderstood so that the victim is blamed for actions or lack of actions.

The community often agrees that the victim was responsible for the abuse. By blaming the victim for something she or he did or did not do, we can fend off the fear we all carry of being vulnerable to harm and unable to avoid it. Victims frequently describe the response of courts and police as a second victimization. They cite many examples where criminal justice officials demonstrate a disturbing lack of awareness of the traumatic effects such events have on the victim.

In many cases there is a connection between the degree of the relationship between *offender* and *victim* and the level of physical aggressive force: typically, less force is used in a close relationship. This does not mean compliance by the person victimized, even if that person is an adult. The assaulting person uses the force needed to achieve his ends. With this mind-set, it is easy for those who offend to minimize and deny the reality of the abuse, particularly if minimal "force" was required.

Such denial is further encouraged by the disparaging way we use terms such as "sex offender" or "child molester," inferring hopeless and utter depravity. It is understandable why persons who offend would want to avoid these labels. I believe people will be better able to take responsibility for what they have done if we clearly name *behaviors* rather than applying heavily loaded labels.

Similarly, those victimized by sexual abuse report difficulty coming to terms with the seriousness of the abuse. Lacking information and a helpful outside perspective, they often direct the anger and confusion at themselves. How does someone who has been victimized obtain a clear understanding of the confusing maze of sexual abuse?

> *Rebecca:* For a woman sitting in a sexual support group, there can be enormous shame. She may even consider herself to be an impostor in the group, if her sexual abuse was "only" verbal, or
> - only happened once, or
> - she was over 18 years of age when it happened, or
> - it was just fondling, or
> - it was a stranger and not a family member, or
> - there was no penetration, . . .
> - and so the list goes on.
>
> I remember thinking, well, at least when this person forced me to do oral sex, *he didn't try to choke me very often.* If I say, "Well, that person had it worse than me," I am using a highly successful denial tool. Unfortunately, many people who use it as a tool have actually had more abuse in their lives that they simply do not remember yet.

Physical Aspects

The physical dimension of sexual abuse is the most visible and superficial effect. When there is a visible injury, a cut, bruise, or mutilation, it is possible to measure the harm and take appropriate medical procedures. I don't use the term *superficial* to mean that the physical effects are unimportant, but because a discussion of the physical damage barely begins to deal with the extent of the harm.

Even so, there can be a great range of physical damage from minor to severe. When an adult penis is forced into a child's vagina, mouth, or anus, the child may have rips, bleeding, and permanent scars. A child might develop a sensitive, reflexive gag response because of forced oral sex. The trauma of rape can be so horrible that the child may lose consciousness from shock and pain and may have a near-death experience.

When sexual abuse does result in physical injury, the injury is sometimes rather easily hidden because genitalia are kept covered. In addition, given the intense shame that victims feel, it is easy to see why so many suffer in silence.

> *Rebecca:* The results of sexual abuse cannot be measured in specific body-part involvement. I agree with what others have said, "Betrayal takes only a minute. A father can slip his fingers into his daughter's underpants in thirty seconds. After that, the world is not the same." [2]

Sexual Aspects

Often when considering the physical aspects of sexual abuse, we first think of physical pain and discomfort. However, abuse can include physical touching that is sexually pleasurable. When the child's body responds physiologically to the pleasuring, further confusion is created. The child may feel betrayed by his or her body. With a limited understanding, the child will be confused about this mixture of trauma and sexual pleasure.

Thus the child will have questions: What does this mean regarding sexual orientation? How does a child sort out the confusion and guilt from a physically pleasurable sensation? The child carries that mix of emotions into adult relationships with harmful results. Iris comments:

> *Iris:* The issue of the ambivalence, the crosscurrents of pleasure sensations and trauma, affected me in this way: What is meant to feel pleasurable is in effect nauseating. I want this, but I feel repelled.

Sometimes the child who has been prematurely and inappropriately engaged in sexual activity becomes an adolescent who seeks affection and comfort by sexually acting out feelings. Family members then focus on the acting-out behavior. I know of instances in Christian families where the victim has been harshly judged and punished for this promiscuity while the root cause of the behavior is not known or is actively denied.

Various studies have shown that a high proportion of prostitutes, both male and female, were sexually abused as children.[3] In many cases, people solicited sexual "favors" from them as children in exchange for candy or privileges. With this conditioning, a logical next step could be providing sexual favors for money.

Adults who were victimized as children report that the abuse had a significant impact on their sexual interest and expression. I spoke with a woman who described how childhood sexual abuse affected her lovemaking with her husband. She explained that certain forms of caressing or touching invoked flashbacks of her grandfather who had abused her. For years she felt guilty about that and blamed herself for not being a "good wife." When she was able to express her anger at the grave of her grandfather and openly discuss with her husband the reasons for her behavior, she experienced some relief from the burden. In such ways, survivors reclaim their sexuality.

Emotional Aspects

How does one respond emotionally to the trauma of sexual abuse? Sometimes the child endures the pain by suppressing events from active memory. Although hidden from conscious memory, the abuse is the cause of considerable confusion and self-doubt; in many situations, the abuse will surface later. Similarly, persons who abuse and know their actions are improper will find ways to cope with that knowledge. They may bury it or reshape it into something different from the original. No matter how the offender explains the sexualized act, the victim knows something is wrong.

That adds to the victim's confusion in a situation, as reflected by a Book Reference Group member:

> *Alexandra:* For me when I was younger, I knew something was wrong because of the way someone acted. We went somewhere and a door got locked. That door didn't get locked other times. That's how I knew. In that situation what I experienced wasn't violent. It didn't hurt me physically, and some of it felt good. But this didn't take away the fact that it felt sneaky, and it felt as if someone was going to catch us. I didn't like it and didn't want to be doing it. For whatever reason, I was going along with it because I liked this person and cared for him.

When children have experiences they cannot understand, they need to find other ways to cope. The child may spend more and more time in a fantasy realm. Some children spend excessive time in an imaginary world; this becomes the norm and continues into adulthood. For those individuals, the intense fantasy process distracts them from their overwhelming emotional pain; on one level, that helps them cope. It also creates psychological confusion; fantasy becomes more real than reality.

> *Alexandra:* I have a sense that not just specific sexual abuse, but all the emotional and psychological trauma during my adolescent years affected my development stages. I don't know for sure, but it feels as if my memory is different from other people. The stress, anxiety, and fear that was happening in my life during that time made certain things [like the sexual abuse] come to the forefront, and I would focus on them, but I could not remember what was happening at school.
>
> When I think about the way I've responded to intense anxiety, I realize it has affected my ability to learn and absorb things. If my anxiety level is up, my body is terrified, and that affects my ability to be objective and to problem-solve.

These comments illustrate that sexual abuse is "psychological warfare," defined by *Webster's Dictionary* (1972) as "the use of psychological means to influence or confuse the thinking, undermine the morale, etc., of an enemy or opponent." When the "enemy" or "opponent" is a trusting child, the impact can be traumatizing indeed.

Such psychological warfare produces a range of emotions from despair to anger and shame. As a child grows up with these confusing and unresolved experiences, she or he will inevitably experience negative repercussions to self-esteem and interpersonal relationships. The individual may internalize the trauma in the form of depression or damaged self-esteem or direct it outward toward others. The latter is the case when persons offend, as confirmed by Gary.

> *Gary:* It may sound melodramatic, but sexual abuse is the end of the world as we know it. It instantly alters the way

we perceive our lives, our surroundings, and our relationships. Everything and everyone is affected. For victims, the world becomes a place of distrust and fear. For offenders, it is a world of intrigue and paranoia. Shame pervades everything.

The effect of sexual abuse is like a scarlet letter, worn not upon the breast, but in the countenance and carriage of offender and victim alike. It is seen in the averted eyes, the inability to fully meet another's gaze. It is a sense, a fear, that everyone knows what has happened, that your secret is written on your forehead. And so it often is. Sexual abuse is guilt, shame, and self-loathing.

There is an immediate sense of isolation and alienation, a feeling that "I am somehow different." For offenders, that feeling may translate to degrading beliefs: "I am disgusting. I am an animal. I am less than human. I am a bad person. I am worthless." These beliefs become dangerous when the behavior becomes the identity of the offender, when the offender perceives himself as beyond redemption, with no hope of attempting to change.

The other side of this perception of being "different" leads to minimization: "I'm just oversexed. It's normal and natural. After all, children have sexual personae." Beyond that, a person who offends may believe that sexual abuse is a "right" or an absolute necessity.

I can attempt a description of what my subjective perceptions were as an offender. I was a marked man, a man who was "different" and who harbored a heavy secret. There was certainly a feeling of exhilaration, a sense of power and control. These were temporary and built on quicksand.

Imagine a sunny day suddenly turned to rain, a steady rain that never stops. Or visualize walking down a narrow hallway in which the walls are tilted. Maintaining one's balance becomes a consuming necessity. That is sexual abuse as I experienced it.

For me, sexual abuse was a trip into fantasy land, an escape from the horrors of daily living that seemed to offer no hope of any kind of fulfillment, a life that was going nowhere. No goals, no advancement, no decent relationships, no real friends. No ambitions or dreams—only fantasies. The pursuit of fantasy became a goal to which I devoted more and more of my waking hours. At the time I didn't really see that the horror of my existence was a direct result of my preoccupation with fantasy.

I became not just a man, but a man with a secret. It's hard to describe the dimensions that secret assumes. It colors everything I did, every action, every perception. In my case, every event came to be sifted through the lens of fantasy, as in a tunnel vision. Every woman became not a person with whom I had a relationship, but a conduit for my fantasy life.

In summary, each of us has a unique history of emotional development and expression. If trauma, sexual or otherwise, has occurred, the individual needs sensitivity to repair the emotional damage carefully and systematically.

Spiritual Aspects

Iris: For me, the sexual abuse created an overwhelming blockage in relating to God, "with heart, soul, mind, and strength," in rejoicing in God with my whole heart, because there were so many holes and empty spaces inside of me.

Abuse is spiritually devastating. Survivors find it difficult to believe in a God who protects and sustains what is just and good when an adult entrusted with their care betrayed them. If an individual has a father who is abusive, the image of God as father can be distressing. What others experience as a symbol of support and nurture becomes a millstone and a hindrance to spirituality for the abused.

We who are committed to the Christian faith may find it difficult to hear of the pain others experience in church life. In our zeal to be ambassadors for the Christian cause, we must not let ourselves be perceived as defensive and reactionary.

Rebecca: Too often when I have spoken about my sexual abuse, these religious people are quick to point out that persons who abused me while proclaiming to be Christian were misinterpreting Scriptures and misusing them. How is a five-year-old child supposed to know that? When you have been programmed as a child with wrongful interpretations, how do you begin to undo the programming? I surely don't know.

The church community's confusion and misinformation about sexual abuse often overshadow the healing, redemptive capacity of faith and the faith community. I have been told that I am too negative and only give examples where the church has failed. More will be said in a later chapter about the healing potential of the church community and the more positive aspects of restoration. However, the purpose here is to uncover the effects of sexual abuse and to underscore that many individuals experience other levels of hurt because the church community does not acknowledge their trauma.

Parents are the child's first teachers and the first models of God. People who have experienced a fundamental betrayal by a parent or parent figure will have difficulty putting their faith and trust in God. These hurting individuals need others to respond with love and caring support. Scripture, when properly quoted in a context, can be a helpful resource for some situations. When the individual is coming to terms with a deep loss of trust or betrayal, it is unlikely that biblical words will be helpful.

More relevant is the biblical exhortation to "weep with those who weep" (Rom. 12:15). There is no antidote or Scripture that can erase childhood years of torment and confusion. Jesus taught us to show love and understanding. Such compassion is a healing balm for someone coping with past abuse. In the same way, love and understanding will be a healing balm when offered to someone who regrets his actions that caused untold pain to others.

The healing balm of the gospel has the power to transform and to make whole. The church has a challenge to truly put faith into practice, to bind up wounds spiritually *and also* physically, sexually, and emotionally.

The effects of abuse are felt, not only by those directly involved and their family and friends, but also by the whole church. Sometimes when I speak to groups about sexual abuse,

I am aware from nonverbal clues that various people are personally affected by what I am saying. In many cases, they are not dealing openly with their issues.

Their pain, even when carried silently, has an impact on the whole community. When "one of the least of these" is harmed, the whole community of faith is wounded and in need of redemption. The need for healing applies as much to the whole church as to the individual. "Bear one another's burdens, and in this way you will fulfill the law of Christ" (Gal. 6:2).

In recent years, courageous persons affected by sexual abuse have begun to share the stories of their abuse and healing in their church communities. It is important that we recognize their offerings as gifts (1 Cor. 12). Whether they are survivors or persons who have offended, they are valued members of the body of Christ, and they need affirmation for the healing gifts they offer.

3

Why Sexual Abuse Takes Place

Then Amnon said to Tamar, "Bring the food into the chamber, so that I may eat from your hand." So Tamar took the cakes she had made, and brought them into the chamber to Amnon her brother. But when she brought them near him to eat, he took hold of her, and said to her, "Come, lie with me, my sister." She answered him, "No, my brother, do not force me; for such a thing is not done in Israel; do not do anything so vile! As for me, where could I carry my shame? And as for you, you would be as one of the scoundrels in Israel. Now therefore, I beg you, speak to the king; for he will not withhold me from you." But he would not listen to her; and being stronger than she, he forced her and lay with her. (2 Sam. 13:10-14)

This passage shows many of the destructive elements of sexual abuse. Amnon had planned that his sister would be vulnerable to his assault. He knew that his actions were wrong and shameful, as did Tamar. But with his greater strength, he forced her and raped her. The Scripture then recounts how this act set in motion a series of violent and destructive acts that affected the whole family.

As this story indicates, sexual abuse has been with us a long time, dating back to the beginnings of recorded history and no doubt even further. As we begin to address sexual abuse, we have many questions: Why does sexual abuse take place? Why does it persist? How does one account for sexual abuse in the religious community? This chapter will discuss such questions by identifying relevant societal and individual factors.

Repressed or Wounded Sexuality

First, there is much confusion and woundedness in our sexuality, as individuals and as a society. Consider these comments from members of the Book Reference Group.[1]

Gary: Why does the individual choose sexual abuse rather than some other outlet for acting out woundedness? Obviously, the question deals with sexuality. Our society has such an ambivalent approach to sexuality, and that ambivalence strikes at the very heart of who we are. Does society not want to look at sexuality? Does it tend not to question too closely what sexuality means to us?

As a society, our whole approach to sexuality is shame-based. This sexual shame may become identified somehow with the whole person. With a shame-based personality, that individual is practically bound to explore or express the depths of that shame in a sexual way.

We are fascinated by what shames us. I feel this as a personal characteristic—the idea that I have sexual desires and needs, even normal ones, causes shame in me, and yet I feel compelled to act in the most shameful and shameless way possible, to heap further shame on myself, to express the addictive "evil" of sexual impulses.

Alexandra: When I consider sexuality in our society, and think about my abuser, my family members, and how they look at sexuality, I think the issue is much bigger than just sexual abuse. I am not minimizing sexual abuse. I think it's a symptom. Some men are not attracted to children or they do not make that step of being sexual with a child, but they may well abuse sex in a different way. I think our distorted views of sexuality are very widespread and have been going on for many long years. It is going to take some doing to change it.

We are constantly bombarded by media portrayals that put an erotic aura around children and make men and women into sex objects. These presentations are evidence of repressed and wounded sexuality. Far from promoting sexual openness, their expression is destructive and inhibiting. Equally hurtful are repressive church teachings about sexuality that invoke guilt and shame.

Alexandra: There is also a lot of confusion between intimacy and sexuality. I feel as if men have more of a challenge because of the way we socialize boys and girls differently. Men are not supposed to be emotional. They are supposed to turn that off. Boys are not supposed to cry, and they are not free to be physically affectionate, except perhaps when playing sports. Are men able to give a nice, long, warm, affectionate hug? My experience of men is that they automatically feel the hug as sexual.

Men are inclined to view touch as sexual. Whatever the origin of this factor, it is important for men to be aware of it and take ownership of it.[2]

Alexandra: I'm not just pointing the finger at men. I know the flip side of the coin, as seen in my own life and in the lives of other women around me. Women have learned that being physically attractive is one way for women to have power. It gets confusing in our society. You learn ways of being seductive as a woman, and I do not mean that as being excessively sexual. I think there are ways of being seductive that women use just as a way of drawing attention. Sexuality issues are widespread and not only specific to those who actually abuse children.

We need to give further thought to men's expression of sexuality. Society conditions men to be the primary initiators of sexual activity; men feel mastery and dominance in that role. In many ways, subtle and direct, our society conveys this message, which becomes part of the belief system of men and women.

When a man is not living up to this role of being sexually

dominant, he can experience great anxiety, performance and otherwise, that contributes to a sense of failure. He directs his accompanying emotions of anger and frustration at those he thinks have caused his anxiety.

> *Alexandra:* My abuser seemed to experience his sexual needs and his sexuality as desperate and uncontrollable. He seemingly couldn't stop himself. It could have been partially a mind game, I don't know, but even my mother believed his sexual needs were out of control. That is part of the whole cultural mess and myth about rape, a myth that says, "Women should not lead men on because men go to a certain point and they cannot control themselves anymore." Not true!

It is essential that we, as a society, hold men responsible for the expression of their sexuality. Otherwise, harmful beliefs remain ingrained, and any change is unlikely.

A man in a counseling session used such a defense to justify himself for forcing sexual activity upon an adult woman. He declared that, by her actions, she had brought him to the "point of no return."

I asked him to imagine that he had crossed his hypothetical point of no return and then to imagine that suddenly the bedroom was on fire. Did he think he could control his sexual expression, or would they perish in the fire? It is important that men hear from men as well as from women that they are responsible for their sexuality.

Patriarchal Values

> *Gary:* I believe the twentieth century has seen the beginning of a significant change in the power relationships of men and women, but not without considerable pain on both sides. This is true for the angry man who sees himself as personally inadequate and powerless. It is also true for men as a group who are feeling under siege as they perceive their power being taken from them by women. The rules are changing, and men are feeling constrained and guarded in both words and gestures. This is very difficult to cope with.

In the Christian church, the term *patriarch* refers to the biblical founding fathers of the Hebrew race: Abraham, Isaac, Jacob, and Jacob's twelve sons. In a patriarchal culture, family membership is traced through males as heads of families and households. Such a culture was in place when the biblical stories occurred and were recorded.

Since biblical times, our social organization has changed dramatically. For example, women and men are now equal under the law, but in biblical times, women had few legal rights and were the legal property of their husbands or fathers. Even today, relics of patriarchy persist. In our society, males and particularly white males clearly have more opportunities and more power over their own lives and destinies. For example, white males can obtain employment more readily and get a higher average income than women or men from minority groups.

The reader may wonder how patriarchy and power relate to sexual abuse. There is a direct relationship. When one group (men) is given greater power, there is a correspondingly decreased examination of their actions. The powerful group is less likely to be held accountable for their actions because they created the very governing institutions that judge them. Many victims say they were discouraged from raising their issues precisely because of these dynamics. Victims are silenced when people say, "He's your father; he wouldn't hurt you." "He's your pastor; you must be making it up."

I am not advocating that all power in relationships be neutralized. Power differences exist and will continue to exist. Parents possess greater resources than their young children, and ideally they use their greater power for the children's good. We may work toward reducing systemic power imbalances such as those between women and men, but the goal is not the elimination of all power differences. With patriarchy, there is a built-in unfair advantage for men based on gender alone. This pervades all of society.

On an individual basis, however, it may appear just the opposite. A man may feel very powerless. He may think he lacks success and prestige when he measures himself against societal expectations of what men "should" be. His frustration and emptiness are significant ingredients in the occurrence of sexual abuse.

> *Gary:* A man who sexually abuses is expressing rebellion against powerlessness, both his own and what he thinks he sees in his relationships and in society.

As a society and as a church community, we must confront issues related to male power, knowing that change causes discomfort, disruption, and conflict.

In a patriarchal system, children are "seen but not heard." Such a belief fosters unhealthy conditions that encourage abuse. Parents need to recognize that the authority of their role carries with it an obligation to perform responsibly and to use their power justly. Too frequently in the past, parents have not used their power to protect and nourish their young.

In our society, children are gaining more power. Today children may leave abusive home situations more readily. While this is healthier for the child, the parents may express great consternation about the way their authority has been undermined. However, the community needs to remind parents that the appropriate exercise of authority includes respectful use of their power.

We have been discussing men who abuse power. When women abuse their power over children or others who are vulnerable, we need to deal with that situation, too.

The Church and Patriarchy

Many Christians believe that male dominance is morally right. Yet the Bible starts out with God commissioning both male and female (Gen. 1:28). Paul teaches mutual submission in marriage out of reverence for Christ (1 Cor. 7:2-4; Eph. 5:21). I wish those who believe in male dominance could spend time with me and see the abuses that result from such a view.

Men must become aware of the power they hold and use because of their gender. Our churches must not teach or support male dominance as a right or a divinely ordained plan.

Such a turnabout will knock out the underpinnings of these harmful beliefs and create healthier families and societies less susceptible to sexual abuse.

One role of institutions is to provide stability and longevity for an organization; in return, institutions respond slowly to changes in society. Because males hold most of the authority positions in church structures and institutions, we have not thoroughly dealt with sexual abuse in the past. Only recently have we begun to see the significance of sexual abuse.

Years ago when churches debated the abolition of slavery, various biblical texts were used to defend slavery as morally correct. Similarly now, Scripture is frequently used to argue for the status quo.

Rebecca discusses the issue of patriarchal dimensions in religious institutions:

> *Rebecca:* I think the whole patriarchal attitude of religion is something that needs to be addressed if we are looking at things from an overall view. Things definitely need to change, and good luck! I was encouraged to hear a workshop speaker say very strongly that things in the churches need to change. She said we are going to have to rework our whole theology.[3] I recognize that it is going to take time. Still, it was great that I actually heard that message in a church!

Change in the church has been painstakingly (and painfully!) slow. One of our immediate tasks is to recognize how institutional structures contribute to our use or misuse of power; we must also continue to challenge the individual misuse of power, whether by males or females.

Gary shares his perspective on the abuse of power:

> *Gary:* I agree that changes need to be made in our patriarchal ways. I'm encouraged when people do make changes. However, I have frequently heard the message, and have at times said myself, that patriarchy is the cause of sexual abuse or encourages it. As we discover more and more women who have offended, this theory will be questioned.

> Perhaps we are now getting down to the basics: sexual abuse arises from how people misuse their power, not from the system itself.

Survivors of sexual abuse and those who have offended sexually have frequently been discouraged by the church's response. They have met many people who were not open to the views and attitudes of those with direct experience.

Members of the Book Reference Group had a variety of involvements in religion, from very active to quite distant. However, none of them were indifferent to the church's role in their abuse. They all responded much like many others with whom I have spoken. They did not see the church as helpful; in most cases, the church was harmful. More recently, I have heard a few encouraging responses when the church has been constructive and supportive.

Corporate Denial

> *Rebecca:* If countries can be in denial that the Holocaust happened, then we know that we are pretty good at mass denial.

Sexual abuse is allowed to occur because we so desperately want it not to happen. We have either completely avoided facing it or have established secretive procedures to handle it privately and sweep it under the rug.

How do secret procedures contribute to more sexual abuse? When the community does not permit information to be shared, there is a greater opportunity for the offending person to continue to operate. The individual may rightly believe that no one other than his victim will know what he is doing. That encourages further abuse. With secrecy, there is no communal agreement to limit the offending person's activities. When the community knows about the abuse, that puts limits on the abuser's freedom to abuse again.

In the church community, this denial may be channeled toward "spiritual victories." Individuals tend to focus their personal sharing on struggles fought and won rather than on issues that they continue to struggle with and fail to overcome. With this desire to live "victoriously," we send signals that it is not acceptable to speak openly of painful, unresolved issues. Because we are silent and uncomfortable with sexuality, we have difficulty talking about such an emotionally charged issue as sexual abuse.

We often call the church the family of God. Members see strong marriages and families as pillars in the church. These are important values to support and nurture in the life of the church community. Churches often have difficulty, however, if the exposure of sexual abuse leads to a marital separation, whether temporary or permanent. Individual family members may be pressured by "shoulds." In such a situation, the emphasis on the values of marriage, family, and church community often buries the deeper issues of sexual abuse and power imbalances. By not working through those volatile issues, we do further harm to individuals as well as to marriages, families, and churches.

Individual Choice and Responsibility

Gary: Without a doubt there is an individual, very personal component to sexual abuse. A facet that we who have offended cannot blame on society, our parents, our upbringing, or our economic and social status. Someplace where, if we are honest, we assume responsibility and say, "I did this; no one forced me into it. From the entire universe of choices, I selected this one."

One person searched for understanding about his own sexual offenses and why he offended:

Jimmy: I keep wondering, "Why did I do it, but the other guy didn't?" Is there something in people's makeup that causes them to abuse? There are so many millions of men who just don't do it, and the rest of us do. Why is that?

Our initial consideration of sexual abuse focused on broader perspectives without looking at individuals. That was deliberate. It is too simplistic to put all the focus on those who are apprehended for sexual offenses without looking at the underlying principles that keep bringing a steady stream of the accused into the courts. It is necessary to consider those broader factors in our society that set the context for the actions of individuals who offend. Does that mean the individual is not responsible? Definitely not.

> *Gary:* On one level, the essence of an offender's recovery and rehabilitation is learning that there is always a choice. Even compulsion offers choices.

Sexually abusive behavior raises contradictory questions:

> *Jimmy:* I don't understand it. Let's say you are a stepfather to a young girl. You love her, even though she is not your own child. If somebody else was going to do something to hurt her, you would fight them and, if need be, die for her. But you still turn around, and the child you are willing to give your life for, to protect, you turn around and hurt her and abuse her.

Other Book Reference Group members responded:

> *Alexandra:* Maybe it's a case of loving her and expressing that love inappropriately. I feel as if there can be all kinds of confusion and difficulty. Your kids are very loving and affectionate and warm, and if you have a need for that because of abuse or a lack in your own life, and here is this wonderful, energetic little being that is all warm and loving and holds onto you and touches you and thinks you are wonderful, it can get really confusing if closeness and affection automatically mean sex to you. I think that those two need to be split apart—the closeness and the sexuality.

> *Gary:* So what makes one a sexual perpetrator rather than acting out in some other way? In my case it was a complex mixture of anger toward women, resentment, sexual shame, family secrets, a sense of powerlessness, and a desire to feel and exert power. There was also a twisted desire to

teach, to banish the sense of shame I felt by acting shamelessly. Probably there are other factors that I still don't know about.

Why Are We Hearing About Abuse Now?

There is no indication that the occurrences of sexual abuse have increased significantly in recent years. However, disclosures have been much more common, giving many the impression that we have an epidemic of sexual abuse. Because there is now a more receptive atmosphere, there is a greater likelihood that silent victims will find their voices and tell of the abuse. On the other hand, there is an increasingly hostile and punitive attitude toward those who have offended; this may inhibit further disclosure.[4]

Sexual abuse was known to exist for many years before it catapulted onto center stage in the early 1980s and gained great attention. Previously, abnormal psychology courses offered it as a topic, suggesting that it was a minor and obscure issue. What changed? Probably the main factor was the women's movement. Before the women's movement, issues of concern for many women were dealt with as secrets or unimportant matters. The same shifts that ushered in the new and liberating perspectives of the women's movement brought abuse issues to the fore.

We are working with sexual offenses that occurred from five, ten, twenty, or even forty years ago and with current abuses. The impact can be overwhelming. Some survivors report sensing that our initial willingness to hear is sometimes retracted, probably because it feels too intense and distressing.

The criminal and civil courts have assisted in this current climate of disclosure by believing survivors' accusations from earlier times. Previous attempts to open up past issues were largely ignored. For some survivors, this forum has provided an avenue to speak their truth and feel some sense of liberation and vindication, after many years of carrying the pain. For others, it is not an appropriate option. If survivors are to open up their abuse wounds, they must be able to exercise some control over if and how their inner pain is expressed.

In earlier times, sexual abuse was not fully identified because the appropriate direct questions were not asked. In many cases, community members did not ask the questions because they did not want to hear the answers. We continue to struggle with this communal denial when we are confronted with forms of sexual abuse that seem incomprehensible, such as women offending. It is imperative that we ask direct and honest questions of both women and men to ensure the protection of our children.

Men as Victims, Women as Offenders

This chapter has discussed societal and individual factors that cause sexual abuse. In most references, it is stated or assumed that the abuser is male and the victim is female. That is not always the case. A significant number of males are sexually abused, and some of their abusers are females.

Male survivors in support groups report that some of their abusers were females. In some cases, they were abused by more than one person during childhood and adolescence, so they may have been abused by both a female and a male.[5] Female survivors who attend groups also identify women as sexual abusers. Those who work with sexual abuse know of enough of these instances to agree that women do offend.

Available information, anecdotal and from research, says women offend less frequently than men. This is probably due to the gender and power factors mentioned earlier. However, for the victims, the pain is just as real and traumatic whether the offender is male or female. Male survivors say they get little support.

Many male victims report strong feelings of shame and guilt. Often they hear or believe that because they are male, they should have "fought to the death" rather than allow a man to perform homosexual acts with them. If the offending person is male, society and even fellow prisoners are likely to become enraged; if female, the abuse is often lightly dismissed. The victim can get a misguided perception that he was just an eight-year-old who "got lucky" when his sixteen-year-old female babysitter made sexual advances. Male victims struggle with confusion between sexuality and sexual abuse. All victims of sexual abuse need the community's full and compassionate response.

False Accusations

Sometimes persons make false claims that crimes were committed. There are instances where persons make false claims about sexual abuse. Law enforcement officials report that very few claims are false accusations. When there is a false complaint, it frequently gets high media coverage. We tend to be excited by bizarre happenings, and this is true in matters of sexual abuse. The extreme and unusual gets disproportionate attention. That makes it more difficult for us to develop a balanced view of the issue.

False accusations of sexual abuse are most likely to occur when there is a high level of conflict between two adults. For example, there may be false accusations in a divorce when a couple is disputing virtually every aspect of their past relationship. Sometimes there is sexual abuse in this kind of situation. It is important not to prejudge and automatically presume that the accusation is false because of the intense conflict between adults.

It is more likely that an adult with some imported theory to prove may influence a child to make a false allegation. It is less likely that an adult or child will, on his or her own, manufacture a completely fictitious account, though occasionally it happens out of spite. Often the offender and victim will disagree on the perspective and details of the offense; it is far less likely that the basis for the claim will be completely false.

To cope with life, many survivors have suppressed their conscious memory of the abuse, often in part because they are living in a household with the offender and may be financially dependent on him. The phenomenon of suppressed memories is difficult for others to comprehend; they may doubt the validity of the survivors' stories as they begin to recall and speak of the abuse. These doubts hurt the victims and inhibit them from giving voice to their trauma.

In another situation, a counselor may assume that the problem relates to past sexual abuse before adequately checking out other possible reasons for the problem.[6] In such a case, the counselor may create in a client a belief that sexual abuse has occurred when it has not. Some people call this "false memory syndrome," a term coined by lawyers defending a person accused of sexual abuse. It refers to a situation where a person fabricates a memory of an event that has not occurred.[7]

So-called false memory syndrome has gained much interest and support and is debated. We certainly must avoid unfounded accusations because of the significant trauma to families affected. At the same time, the keen interest in false accusations can be a new way for the accused to avoid responsibility and a convenient way for society to avoid facing the reality of sexual abuse.

Concern about this issue has led to greater exploration of memory and how it works. It has also caused counselors to examine their techniques more diligently, to ensure that their methods do not create problems instead of solving them.

Conclusion

There is no easy or complete answer about why one person sexually abuses another. Similarly, it is difficult to understand why there is abuse from generation to generation. There are, however, clues that point us to things we must change if we are to work toward eliminating sexual abuse in our society.

More will be said later about ways to stop the cycle of abuse. For a start, we must recognize that the problem exists and talk about it in an open and respectful way that involves everyone affected. Sexual abuse is an issue that is imbedded in many layers of our communities, churches, and families. We cannot expect that sudden, dramatic steps will immediately eradicate all abuse. Instead, we can commit ourselves to taking gradual and incremental steps that move us toward healing.

4

Restorative Justice

My experience with the criminal justice system began in 1969. Fresh out of university, I began a full-time voluntary service assignment with a local probation office. The church agency I served prescribed my goal—to find ways for persons from the church community to get more involved in the criminal justice system.

I clearly remember my early impressions of the courts and the many people I saw involved there, the stilted formality of the courtroom, and the lengthy discussions by court officials over what appeared to be trivial details. Besides meeting the "clientele" of the system, I had a unique opportunity to interact with the courtroom officials. The police, prosecuting attorneys, and judges seemed austere in the courtroom setting, but they were quite personable in one-to-one situations. *Why do they seem so cool and detached in the courtroom?* I wondered.

As I learned more about the court system with its rules and procedures, I felt less overwhelmed and more able to understand. I adjusted my expectations of a sentence pronounced by the judge, for example, by learning what was typical for such an offense. I adapted to the environment and accepted the basic assumptions of that system without serious questions.

After this experience with the court system, I met with a group of individuals from various churches who were interested in some form of involvement in the criminal justice system. I explained various aspects of this formidable system of justice.

As a full-time probation officer, I continued to work with people from the churches in a program to match persons on probation with community volunteers. I was intrigued by the energy and commitment of the volunteers. Other probation officers also expressed interest in the volunteers.

In 1974, I discussed a court case with this group of volunteers. Two young men had gone on a rampage in the town of Elmira, Ontario, slashing tires, breaking windows, and generally destroying anything in their path. This resulted in twenty-two criminal charges for property damage. As a probation officer, it was my task to prepare a presentence report to give the court background information about the accused.

I casually suggested, "Wouldn't it be interesting for these guys to meet with their victims?" I thought, *It's safe to say that to a group that has little involvement in the criminal justice system.* Their response surprised and challenged me: "Yes, arrange for the young men to meet their victims!"

By this time I had had enough experience with the courts to know that such things did not happen. It was just not done. There were two sides, the victim and the offender, and they had no contact with each other. As a probation officer, I almost never spoke to the victims of crimes. I only interacted with those who were convicted of offenses. The system was not organized for encouraging those who committed crimes to actually meet and interact with their victims.

One member of the group, Dave Worth, then a full-time church volunteer, accompanied me to talk with the presiding judge. Again, I was surprised. The judge initially responded that our request was unusual. Then he quickly gave his approval for the accused to meet their victims and to determine with them what restitution or repayment was required. The process was underway.

Accompanied by Dave Worth or me, the two young men retraced their steps of that fateful evening and introduced themselves to the affected people at the front doors of their homes. The victims' responses were varied. Consistently they deplored the young men's destructive acts and expressed appreciation for the fact that they were taking ownership and facing what they had done. They often talked about the fear and inconvenience they had experienced as a result of the vandalism.

In a few cases, the victims asked for the young men's last names a second time, and then inquired about possible connections to persons they knew by the same family name. As requested by the judge, the two young men asked about their victims' expenses and the portion that had been covered by insurance.

After the two earned the restitution money, they returned with a certified check for each person. This time, the young men were more confident. They eagerly knocked on the doors and handed people their checks. The compensated victims commended the young men. The picture window in one woman's living room had been broken with a rock. She commented, "This $100 check is money I had not expected to receive; it's a gift to me. I'm going to pass it on to help others in need."

Thus the Victim-Offender Reconciliation Program (VORP) began in Canada, and the movement spread to the USA a few years later. Through this experiment, I learned a lot about how the interaction of community people can bring change to those inside the system and those outside the system. Because I was a member of the court system, I did not see opportunities for innovation. I was restricted by my sense of what would be consistent with the judicial system.

Dave Worth and others did not know the court system, but they had a firm vision for what should happen and faith in the process for making that vision come true. Since they didn't know that having victims meet their offenders was "impossible," they lobbied to make it happen. In this case, as in many others, change comes when individuals look outside the traditional limits to resolve complex problems.

This first victim-offender mediation returned the conflict to the people directly affected. This contrasts sharply with the usual process, where ways of resolving conflicts and righting wrongs are formalized and taken out of the hands of those most involved. The procedures are removed from their human elements, and the resolutions are remote, arbitrary, and unsatisfying. We, however, encourage the wrongdoer to take responsibility, in a problem-solving rather than a blaming mode. Thus we can anticipate a more complete sense of justice, not only for the wrongdoer, but also for victims and others who were hurt.

Jesus said his followers are "in the world, but not of the world" (John 17:15-16). This understanding is important to my Mennonite faith community. It is a way of expressing the Christian's nonconformity to the *world*—defined as all that is against God and is not church. To describe my approach to the criminal courts, I use an adapted phrase: "in the system, but not of the system." Our Lord calls us to bring Christian values and beliefs to bear on this secular system. At the same time, it is essential for me to detach from the system enough to allow catalysts to cause change. From this value base and set of experiences, I begin to describe "restorative justice."

Restorative Justice—An Alternative to Punishment and Rehabilitation

While visiting a neighborhood park, I stood on a bridge, looking at my reflection in the still water below. Suddenly a squirrel dropped a walnut from a tree branch overhead. It broke the calmness of the water.

Where the walnut hit the surface, the water erupted and a series of symmetrical ripples momentarily disrupted the surface. Soon the water absorbed the impact of the walnut, and its peaceful mirror-like surface returned. *How did the water absorb the impact of the walnut?* I wondered. *What about the bottom of the lake? Is that disruption continuing beneath the tranquil surface of the water?*

Crime impacts our community and society like ripples breaking the water's smooth surface. When a crime disturbs the peace of our community life, too often we try to contain the eruption, the most obvious outcome of the event. We give little time or effort to understand the impact of the resulting ripples or to take care of the effects beneath the surface. As a society we spend too much time and energy trying to understand and correct the walnut (offender); we do not give enough attention to the water (victims) affected by the walnut.

If we hope to respond to crime in a restorative manner, we must broaden our view of what is important. We need to look beyond the disruption of the smooth surface of the water and attend to the underwater surges as well. We need a new pattern for looking at old problems, a model that changes the way we see harm and its impact on the community. Using a new model can bring deeper levels of healing to our communities.[1]

Traditionally we have responded to persons whose actions cause ripples within the community in one of two ways. First, the person who offended is viewed as obviously bad, so *punishment* is required. The purpose of the punishment is to show the wrongdoer that something is being done to deal with the situation, to tell him that he can't do that and get away with it. It shows the victim that the offender is being held accountable for his actions.

Because of the punishment, others may be deterred from such offenses, or the offender might change his behavior, which is good. Primarily, though, the punishment is intended to overcome the imbalance created by the harmful act, to create a new balance.

An alternative response developed that changed the focus from punishment to *rehabilitation* of the offender. In this view, the offending person is mad or deranged because of previous life experience, and the correct response is rehabilitation. The wrongdoer is not at heart a bad person. He was shaped by destructive surroundings and needs therapeutic treatment and rehabilitation. Such rehabilitation will bring the person to acknowledge past wrongdoing and, we hope, avoid committing further wrongful acts.

In spite of their differences, both interpretations suggest that something is wrong with the offender; both are pessimistic about the offender's ability to change. In both perspectives, victims and the community are excluded and watch from the sidelines. The focus is on the individual offender.

Restorative justice offers a third perspective, to make community whole again. It does not focus on punishment or rehabilitation merely of the offender. Instead, it works more broadly, for *responsibility* in the community. Criminal actions are symbols that the wrongdoers are disconnected from broader society. Those actions further disrupt community for the offenders and others. Restorative justice seeks to restore those who offend to their communities, to restore the sense of community for those who have been victimized, and to repair the damaged community fabric.

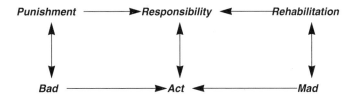

Those who respond to crime using the restorative justice model attempt to recognize and meet the needs of victims and offenders and the community at large. The wrongdoer is held accountable and is supported in taking responsibility for specific wrongful acts. Simultaneously, victims and others affected by the crime are offered support and aid for healing. This involves responding to the ripples of the crime above and below the surface. It means allowing all those affected to become part of the problem-solving process, so the community is more likely to experience restoration.

A medical analogy helps to illustrate. If someone has a contagious disease, that person will be isolated while getting treatment for the disease. The isolation protects others in the community. A person with a "social disease" is already not well connected to the community. In the case of a sexual offender, the diseased (bad or mad) person is similarly isolated. But such treatment, though it temporarily protects victims, in the long run makes the problem worse rather than healing the offender or the community.

Restorative justice does not see the person himself as diseased but rather as acting out of isolation or alienation. He indeed may have many social connections but misuse some of them for his own sexual gratification. Thus he or she needs to be joined or integrated into the community again in healthy and not in exploitative ways. The offending person needs to be involved in the problem-solving process, as do the victim or victim's representatives and community persons; in this way the community is repaired. Restorative justice provides safety for all while working toward reconnecting the offending person with the community. It helps the community function in a more integrated way.

The key step is encouraging the offending person to take responsibility for his harmful actions. Unfortunately, those who support persons who have offended frequently do just the opposite. In a misguided attempt to help them cope with the aftermath of what they have done, the "supporters" minimize the personal responsibility of those who have offended. Ironically, they tend to shift blame to the victims. Often community members lay on victim-survivors the responsibility for ensuring that there are no further offenses. They may even chastise victim-survivors for their course of action or for even lodging complaints.

> *Rebecca:* I really resent the guilt that is laid on me by some people because I don't take my brother to court. As far as I am concerned, his wife knows, the entire family knows, but to some people, it's still my responsibility.

Assumptions Underlying Restorative Justice

To understand restorative justice fully, we must give further attention to three essential elements: the victim perspective, the offender perspective, and the community perspective. We will consider various aspects of these three perspectives and their interconnections.[2]

Victim Perspectives

Frequently people who have been harmed by the deliberate acts of another find their sense of safety and security has been shaken. Often they don't know how their grievance is being handled by the broader community, whether in family, church, or court. This is isolating and disturbing for crime victims. No matter how the wrong is being handled, it is essential that the victim have as active a role as the victim desires in seeing the process through to completion. Victims experience more healing if they believe the process has led to a satisfactory conclusion.

Victims also need to have others acknowledge the harm that has been done to them. Our criminal justice system tends to handle this part superficially and insensitively, if at all. In many ways, victims are pushed to move on. Such pressure is not helpful; it actually increases the harm.

When considering the victim, we must broaden our understanding to include secondary victims. Victim ripples often affect many other persons. If the aftereffects of wrongdoing are to be addressed wholistically, we must consider as many of these individuals as realistically possible.

Family members are usually affected significantly when a member of their family has been harmed. If the abuser is a family member or a close friend, there are added complications and divisions. Such families need support as they attempt to respond to the victim with care.

Secondary victims can include family members (particularly a spouse), parents, children, co-workers, friends, and others from the church community. They may hurt in varying degrees. To be healed, they need help in working through the pain.

Offender Perspectives

If we are to work toward justice and healing, we need to understand the perspective of the offenders. It is often hard for us to see their pain because we are repelled by their actions and defensiveness. Nevertheless, we must separate the person from the wrongful acts if we are to be restorative. We can create a society more free of sexual abuse and other offenses only if we separate our distaste for a person's actions from our compassionate response to such an individual. Otherwise, our efforts are counterproductive.

When we are genuinely concerned for persons who have offended, we can give response to them honestly and share our perspectives about their behavior openly. As shown in following chapters, it is important to balance support with confrontation. Over time, the offending person can understand the extent of harm caused by the wrongful acts. The most common shortcoming of helpers is to move away from the dual responses of support and challenge too quickly. Those who have offended need *steady confrontation and supportive challenge* to allow their newly developed behaviors to take root and become the norm.

An important aspect of restorative justice is *restitution*. This means providing opportunity for the person who offended to give something back, to make some form of payment for the harm done. It is a symbolic action because in many cases it is difficult or impossible to restore fully what has been damaged. The wrong cannot be undone, but restitution is important in healing each individual and in restoring community. It is valuable to seek restitution and to take appropriate steps toward it, as explained below.

Restorative justice provides avenues for those who have offended to contribute to a fuller understanding of the issue. Jimmy, a member of the Book Reference Group, describes his change in attitude:

> *Jimmy:* I feel a hundred times better than when I came into the program. I feel uplifted. I feel good about myself. I guess one of the things is that I felt so badly about what I did. I felt shame. If I can give something back, it takes away some of the shame. That's how I see it. If I keep giving back, the shame will be less.

Jimmy has developed a comprehensive list of strategies that persons use when offending sexually, and he shares that list with offender and community groups.[3] In this example, one individual has made a positive contribution toward a fuller understanding of sexual abuse. He hopes this information will help to end sexual abuse.

As we consider offender perspectives, we also need to take into account the family members and other support persons who are secondary victims. Recently a man began talking to me in the washroom after I made a presentation about criminal justice issues at a church conference. He made a few casual comments and then shared his personal pain about his son, an offender. "If my son died," he sadly said, "people would mourn his passing. But now no one says anything. I know people read the newspapers and are aware of my son's offenses, but nobody talks to me about it."

While dealing with the concerns of victims and offenders, we must also face the anguish of those whose hopes and dreams for a son or daughter have been shattered, replaced by shame and guilt. In addition, siblings suffer when family members abuse others. If the person who offends is married or has children, more are affected. The ripples go on and on, and those caught in the waves cope as well as they can. The church community has a valuable opportunity to listen and acknowledge the pain and loss.

Community Perspectives

The community absorbs the trauma of hurtful events in a variety of ways. To return to the earlier metaphor, just because the circles in the water disappear, that does not mean that the aftereffects are gone. Over the centuries, communities have developed mechanisms to cope with harmful actions. As society has become more complex and professionalized, the responses to crime have become more formal, with less informal community involvement. There is less opportunity for those most affected by the crime to have any significant role in responding to the crime or in bringing about justice.

In principle, restorative justice wants the community to have ownership of the conflicts that divide it. It is not an anti-professional stance. However, restorative justice advocates would like to reverse the trend toward assuming that those who are professionally trained to address issues of law, problem solving, and therapy should handle everything. That system keeps the community from having a meaningful role in resolving the conflict.

The current system gives professionals rather than those most affected the responsibility for doing something about the pain and disruption of the community. They respond to the crime in a formal, structured manner. In the restorative justice model, professionals use their expertise to empower families and communities to work through painful issues. Such a partnership of professionals and community will achieve effective and meaningful responses to crime.

The court system is the most formalized community process that responds to sexual abuse. Abuse is processed through a complicated set of guidelines and procedures. Ultimately, it comes before a community representative called a judge, who arbitrates the dispute. Sometimes a jury is included, to represent community peers.

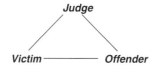

As the community's representative, the judge is at the top of the triangle and holds the power to make decisions. The judge controls the process. By representing society's interests, the judge offers a perspective beyond the roles of the two parties before the court. The judge also tries to use his influence to deter destructive behavior in the broader community.

The victim's interests in a criminal trial are represented by a prosecutor who actually represents the "people's" or the "crown's" interests, which means the larger community. Often the accused will also have a professional to represent her or his interests. When the lawyers for the state, the lawyers for the offender, and the judge communicate, they must follow formal rules. Those rules make it less likely that helpful communication will take place. Direct interaction between victim and offender is almost nonexistent. Other community representatives can be involved only if they present information directly connected to the court case.

The focus is on an event described as a "charge." Only matters related to that event are considered relevant. This strict process seems to cut this one event out of the fabric of what is often a long-term relationship, put it under a magnifying glass, and give it intense scrutiny. The goal is to "prove beyond reasonable doubt" the guilt of the person charged.

This approach has some advantages. It can be affirming for a victim to receive the court's validation of the harm done. Sometimes, particularly where there has been spousal abuse or sexual abuse, it may be one of the few public settings where a victim feels safe enough to talk about the violation. As a public process, it can focus society's attention on the prevalent issues in the community. Indirectly, the community is encouraged to make commitments toward prevention. Finally, an uncooperative offender can ignore community accountability structures, but the court has the authority to place restrictions backed up by the force of law.

I do not wish to argue for the elimination of this method or to discourage persons from using it. Instead, I hope we will develop and encourage a variety of options that give greater choice to victims and other community members as they search for justice.[4]

In some instances, the courts can be used in conjunction with other approaches, such as the Victim-Offender Reconciliation Program (VORP). This brings a broader and more comprehensive dimension to problem solving.

Many persons believe the triangle model described above does not pick up their concerns and solve problems in a healing manner. Its formality is intimidating and disillusioning. Frequently victims describe the court process as a second victimization. To force the state to present its case for scrutiny, the accused must not admit responsibility. In many cases, however, a guilty plea avoids a trial but allows little opportunity for the parties most affected to influence the outcome.

The triangle model also frequently permits the offender to legally agree to the charge without actually taking any responsibility. Many persons convicted by a court can provide a variety of explanations about why they pled guilty to the charge, even though they "didn't really do it."

For strategic legal reasons, a lawyer may advise the accused to plead "not guilty," whether or not the accused did what is alleged. This legal posturing sends a powerful message to the victim(s) that is often devastating.

In recent years new procedures allow greater input from victims and their families through victim-impact statements at the time of sentencing. This gives victims a forum where they can be heard and have some influence on the sentence to be imposed.

The earlier diagram showed the division between punishment and rehabilitation. Whether the approach is to punish or to rehabilitate, many assume that a sentence of time removed from the community does deal with the harm caused. This sanction has been used repeatedly for increasingly long periods of time. Yet it is disturbingly clear that such an approach does not aid in prevention and does not help those most affected to heal.

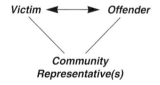

Let us invert the previous justice triangle and place the victim and offender at the top, with the community representative(s) at the bottom. The victim and offender are encouraged to have dialogue and interaction. The community representatives facilitate and set the boundaries. Then a different process is set in motion.

Community representatives and family members who have

relationships with both parties and provide support for both parties play an important role in absorbing the ripples set in motion by the wrongful act. Such an approach does not ignore or suppress the damage. Instead, it allows all those affected an opportunity to address the harm and restore the community.

Sometimes family members who support someone who has offended can hear the depth of hurt and harm caused more clearly than the offender can. The offender may be too self-absorbed and defensive to comprehend it fully. If that is the case, then those supporters can on an ongoing basis provide an appropriate balance of compassion and challenge.

Conclusion

Frequently new ideas emerge in response to dissatisfaction with what currently exists. The criminal justice system has become alienating for most persons associated with it. This chapter provides a stimulus for people to create a renewed sense of making justice. One of these new ways is referred to as restorative justice. Following chapters will apply restorative justice principles to a variety of settings and situations.

5

Applying Restorative Justice

James arrived on time for our first appointment. I was struck by his rugged good looks and the deep frown on his forehead. That frown made the thirty-nine-year-old look as though he were carrying the weight of the world on his shoulders. He had been abrupt on the phone, responding "yes" to my inquiries about why he wished to see me: "Does it involve a sexual matter? Have charges been laid? Is the victim a family member or close relative?"

We were meeting to decide whether he would become involved in a group program for persons who had offended sexually. I asked him if he had any questions to ask me before we began. He shook his head with an expression of mixed feelings. On the one hand, he seemed to be saying, "Let's get on with it," and on the other, "I really don't want to be here."

"Honesty and openness are key steps in beginning the healing process," I began. "What we say is confidential and will not be shared beyond our agency without your permission." I described the limits of my offer of confidentiality. "However, if during your sharing, matters are raised which show that children presently minors have been harmed or are at risk of harm, I will discuss with you the way such information will be shared with child protection authorities."

Sometimes such a statement raises concerns, but not for

James. He said he was aware of what the law said in this regard and was ready to go on. "The purpose of this meeting is to have you share as honestly and openly as possible about the matters that bring you here," I repeated. "I know that's not easy. The prospect of talking about sexual impropriety with someone you have just met has to be rather scary."

He nodded, and tears welled up in his eyes, ever so slightly. I continued: "I will be asking you many specific questions. Some of them, particularly dealing with your sexual offenses, will be on matters you are probably not very comfortable talking about. That is understandable and to be expected.

"If there are matters you don't feel at ease in talking about now, just indicate that. We can go back to it another time. I'd much rather go back to questions you're uncomfortable with than to have you hesitate or give incomplete and inaccurate information. Does that make sense?" He again nodded and added that he has always tried to be truthful.

"How are we doing so far?" I asked.

He smiled and took a sip of coffee before replying. "I'm sure I'll be okay once we get going, but getting started is always hard."

"That's understandable," I said. "How would you like to begin? Do you prefer to share your story surrounding the matter that brings you here, or is it easier if I ask questions?"

James leaned forward and began to speak in a somewhat halting manner:

> I'm not at all aggressive. I would never hurt anyone sexually or otherwise. That's why it's so hard to understand what happened with Julie [his eleven-year-old stepdaughter]. I would never have continued to do the things I was doing if she had said no. Now that I'm not allowed to see her, it makes it impossible for us to work things out. Can't you talk to the authorities and convince them that our case is different? I really think I can help Julie come out of this without much hurt, but they've got to let me speak to her.

I paused briefly before responding to his question. I wanted to tell him many things: that his case was not unique; that part of what he needed to face was his development of an inappropriate relationship with his child; that it was going to be far more complicated to unravel the harm he had done to his child than he could imagine. However, experience has taught me that debating these points is usually not successful.

I told James that I would not contact the authorities, because he was too close to the situation to be effective in assisting his daughter or the family now. I returned to the points he had raised: "You can best help your family by facing your own issues. Are you prepared to do that?" With more clarification, he agreed that he was. Then I asked him to tell me about how he experienced his family as he was growing up.

> *James:* We had a pretty good family, except for my dad. He never smoked or drank, nothing like that, but I could never measure up. I always felt judged by him, especially when he quoted Scripture to me. He was a deacon at church and chairman of the building committee for the new addition. After the plaque went on the wall with his name on it, I never went back to the church.

I invite the reader to think for a moment. From what you have heard so far, what is your impression of James? If you have little sympathy for his situation, your response is typical. He obviously wants to explain away and minimize his sexual assaults of a child. You may acknowledge that he has some past hurts, but who hasn't had some kind of childhood pain? His personal pain is not an excuse for his sexual abuse.

It is easy to respond with anger and a desire to avenge the hurt. Alternatively, we may remember that God commanded us to forgive, and so we must comply. Both responses assume that one quick reaction effectively addresses the multilayered hurt of sexual abuse. In my experience, the alternative known as restorative justice (described in chapter 4) is a more effective way to deal with crimes committed by one person against another.

A central point of restorative justice is trying to understand the wrongful acts as seen by all the persons affected by those acts. As stated in chapter 4, we must take into account the perspectives of victim, offender, and community. Our goal is to deal with the wrongful act(s) in a way that provides all affected persons with paths toward healing, while not losing sight of the consequences that follow such behavior. Let's apply this approach to the victim.

Julie's contact with her natural father had ended when her mother left the family home with Julie and her younger brother, seeking safety in a women's shelter. Julie was six years old when her mother first began to live with James. After living alone for more than a year, the mother told Julie and her brother, Greg, that "Uncle James" was going to live with them, and she planned to marry him.

Uncle James had come over for occasional visits. Julie liked him because he took an interest in her. She was gradually beginning to trust him. He did not have the violent outbursts that Daddy used to have. Julie remembered the time she had spilled the milk she was pouring on her cereal. She still could visualize Daddy's large hand striking her and hear his angry, mean words.

Uncle James seemed so kind and often brought her candy when he visited. She liked to snuggle up on his lap, and at first she felt secure there. After he moved in, she became increasingly uncomfortable with his touch; his kisses became gradually longer and more lingering. Julie did not talk to her mother about her discomfort. Her mom seemed happier than she had been in a long time, and Greg often played catch with Uncle James and actually called him Daddy!

When her mom's hours at work shifted so she worked until ten most evenings, Uncle James put Julie to bed. Julie couldn't remember when he stopped reading bedtime stories and introduced her to "Daddy and Julie's little secret." She only knew that when he rubbed between her legs, it gave her a strange nice feeling, but it also made her feel dirty and ashamed.

To cope with her strong feelings during the abuse, Julie focused her attention on a loose piece of wallpaper bulging from her bedroom ceiling. She imagined herself crawling in behind the wallpaper and watching what Uncle James was doing to her body. For four years, the sexual abuse continued on at least a weekly basis. Through it all, Julie kept her placid smile. She thought if she resisted, Uncle James might become angry and hit her as her daddy used to do. She did the only thing she knew how to do in the circumstances: she suffered in silence, and life went on.

Julie's perspective may raise questions for some readers: Why didn't she tell someone? How can we be sure she did not imagine some of the activity? Before we respond, it's important to recognize our own difficulty in accepting the reality of sexual abuse as experienced by many children. Because of such reluctance, we respond in ways that indirectly or openly say that the victim was responsible for the abuse and for not stopping it.

Julie's mother, Rachel, is another person affected by the wrong. She had to consider how to respond to the crisis. When the guidance teacher asked her to come to the school immediately, she was not prepared for what she heard. How could she not have been aware, if this was really happening? What would her family think of her? She was obviously a complete failure in marriage. First she married a man who was a "Christian" but abused her. Now she was in a marriage where her husband sexually abused her child.

However, Julie's fearful and tearful words pushed Rachel past her own concerns to acknowledge her daughter's trauma—the unthinkable had indeed happened. She instinctively called her pastor, who had been so supportive in her past crises.

Pastor Cooke was shocked by her call. He met with her immediately and asked if there wasn't some mistake or misunderstanding. He reminded Rachel that less than a year ago, Julie had been caught stealing candy; at first she had strongly denied it. Perhaps this was a similar situation.

Other factors affected Pastor Cooke's response. He had supported Rachel in her decision to end the physically abusive relationship with her first husband. Many in the church didn't understand or approve of the way he handled that situation. When Rachel met James and decided to marry him, Pastor

Cooke had provided premarital counseling. He had given church membership instruction to James before he joined the church.

Pastor Cooke had put himself on the line to support James. How could he have been so wrong about him? He began to question his own ability and judgment as a pastor. If he was so wrong in this case, were his assessments so far off the mark in other situations?

As Rachel sat across from him in tears over her discovery, the pastor decided to remain objective and professional. He tried to be an empathetic listener for his parishioner, without giving further indication of his doubts and personal struggles.

Rachel found his response unhelpful. She heard him doubt Julie's honesty (the episode of lying about stealing candy), and she had some questions of her own even though she now fundamentally believed Julie. But she hesitated to share those questions lest they undermine Julie and too readily be accepted as reality. Later she decided the pastor could have helped her more by disclosing some of his further doubts. Nevertheless, he did offer her support in her effort to work through the problems.

Others were directly affected by the issue of sexual abuse in the immediate or extended family. In this example, imagine the impact on Julie's brother, Greg. If Greg had a positive relationship with his stepfather, James, he might resent his sister. Her disclosure also affected him, causing restrictions on a relationship that provided him with significant support.

Also affected were friends and co-workers of both Rachel and James, Julie's friends, school officials, and church members. All these persons and others became aware of what had happened. They interpreted the events based in part on their own experiences and sometimes on their previous views of the persons involved.

The police spoke with James, and he acknowledged that he had sexually abused Julie. That helped to clarify the issue for various persons affected and made it possible to move toward a resolution. One can only guess what would have happened if James had tried to capitalize on the doubts of some people. In many cases when the perpetrator denies the abuse, it is related in part to the way other family members deny anything so unpleasant. We are in a much better position to work for healing when offenders acknowledge the problem. Then we can work together toward a solution.

In the above scenario, when the matter was reported to the authorities, it was brought into the open and handled. James acknowledged what he did. In many cases, families tend to minimize or totally deny the abuse. If that had developed, it would have placed Julie in a precarious situation. Imagine her deep sense of betrayal and despair.

Similarly, consider the results if the abuse had been covered up and ignored. Julie might have grown up and seemed to function quite well academically, continuing to live at home as part of the family. Such an issue festering over a period of years would have had a profound impact on her in later life.

If she married, her husband, with or without foreknowledge, could have become another victim of the abuse. Frequently I have spoken to women and men whose partners experienced sexual abuse. I have heard their expressions of confusion and aloneness in grappling with dimensions that they could not face and rectify. One partner described it as "shadow boxing with a known but unseen adversary."

Applying Restorative Justice to Sexual Abuse

When restorative justice principles are applied to sexual abuse issues, it is important to be aware of the dynamics in such situations.[1] Sometimes in our efforts to be innovative and creative, we fail to focus on the whole system, on the broader issues that are relevant. I frequently quote a proverb: "Let those who wish to make things better, beware, lest they make them worse!" (compare Luke 11:24-26 and the physicians' pledge to do no harm).

The traditional justice system does have built-in mechanisms to protect victims who go through the proper legal procedures. Many do not wish to use that formal system more than legally required, as for sexual abuse of children. They try to handle sexual abuse issues in alternate and less formal ways. Before bypassing formal safeguards, however, we all must shift our thinking. This change of thought patterns needs to be done by offender and victim, and just as urgently by their respective circles of support. If these communities in any way minimize or condone the wrongful acts, they lose the central ingredient for handling such matters.

At the heart of restorative justice is the belief that justice requires dealing with the relationship between victim and offender. If that relationship involved sexual abuse and the accompanying abuse of power by the offender, we need to consider additional factors. The attempt to provide restorative justice should not pressure the victim so he or she feels abused by the process and withdraws.

When victim and offender are part of the same family, extended family, or church community, another dimension is added. Our family norms suggest handling problems quietly, almost privately. Families don't want to "air their dirty laundry in public." Such secrecy usually takes power away from the victims. In most cases, it also does not help those who offend because it makes the offense seem less serious than it really is. The offender is not required to face the agony he has caused so many people.

At the same time, we must hear the victim and respect the victim's need for feeling safe. There cannot be an authentic restored relationship until the victim has reestablished trust in the offender. The victim may trust him after a long time or never trust him. Reestablishing trust does not depend only on the victim. It also depends on the offender's actions after the offense and on the community acting to hold the offender accountable. Often some accountability structure is needed to monitor the one who has sexually offended for the rest of his life. More will be said on this matter in chapter 9, on forgiveness.

Restorative Justice in the Case Example

Gary: To me, restorative justice is a variety of things. It means looking at both sides of the issue, not just at the

offender's side. It includes a sense of self-respect for survivor and offender. It is a restoration to health. With respect
to sexual abuse, justice ultimately comes with the restoration of the people most directly involved. The community
has a role in facilitating that.

As our report about James illustrates, one case of sexual
abuse affects many people. Many ripples are recognized when
applying restorative principles. This section provides practical
guidelines for applying restorative justice principles. It is
beyond the scope of this book to provide a full outline of a
treatment plan for sexual abuse. Some of what follows is common to other treatment approaches, yet it is important to
remember the principles of restorative justice that underlie
these remarks. Throughout, it is essential to treat all involved
persons with respect.

Working with Others

Restorative justice attempts to repair relationships; this
involves seeking out and working with others. We carefully consider how we work with other agencies that may have a man-
dated role. For example, if the sexual abuse occurred recently,
the family will be involved with a child protection agency and
likely with the police as well. Our openness to working with
other agencies is respectful and helps us to avoid falling into the
trap of feeling superior because of our high values.

Often individuals want to deal with the matter without
police or court involvement. While this approach can provide
more latitude to address the issues, it also calls for a heavy
responsibility to manage a complex matter. In some cases this
will be beyond the capability of persons involved. Furthermore,
in most of North America, child sexual abuse must be reported
to the authorities; professionals who break these laws are punished.

If legal authorities are not called in, the victim is usually
pressured to resolve the matter quickly and quietly. Those managing the process may not insist on fundamental changes by the
person who offended. Rob puts the matter this way:

> *Rob:* I think sometimes the courts and even jail have a very positive role to play as a wake-up call. It worked that way for me.

Without the external control of a court order, James, for example, may prematurely insist on contact with Julie. He may decide, after a few months in a remedial program, that he understands what he has done and that he will not re-offend. Then he may discontinue group involvement and individual counseling. His network will likely not provide sufficient support to ensure that James fully understands his problem, takes responsibility for what he has done, and makes the major changes in his life that might lead to restoration.

Therefore, external control is essential. At the same time, it is important to recognize that external control must become the individual's self-control over time. Otherwise, the community will need to monitor that individual on an ongoing basis.

A child protection agency is authorized to protect children. In the past when sexual abuse was identified, the family remained together and was sent to counseling. Because of many cases where the pattern of abuse continued during and in spite of the process, agencies became convinced that a more fundamental change is required. If a father or stepfather is the abuser, he must be separated from the family for a time to break the power dynamics and control that he as a parent exercised in a destructive manner. Consequently, his future as a parent may be tenuous and limited.

When the perpetrator is denied access to the child victim, he may direct considerable anger and frustration toward the authorities. Often he or his supporters will condemn the child protection agencies for breaking up the family. At times, individual social workers may be overzealous. Nevertheless, agencies do have an obligation to ensure that children are protected.

Confronting and Supporting Restoratively

Productive work cannot begin until James feels trust. James must feel confident that he can safely open up his past secrets before he will begin to disclose them in a meaningful way. He needs others who offer him honesty and an open approach, who explain what is happening and why, and who respect his initial reluctance to share very private matters.

While establishing trust is essential, the listener must guard against joining forces with James. I know how hard it is to hear the anguish of most persons who offend without developing a sense of empathy. Some listeners may manage their own discomfort by concluding that James's abuse of his stepdaughter was minor. Thus they unwittingly help James minimize the events and blame the victim. That is why it is so important to have information about the perspective of the victim.

It is important to provide a balance between support and confrontation. You can truly confront only to the degree that you can also support. On the graph, insofar as you can support on the one hand, you can also confront with integrity. If you support without confronting, you join the offender in his refusal to change and grow. If you confront without corresponding support, James will maintain his walls of defensiveness and block out any significant impact to produce change.

Confrontation ◄──────────────► *Support*

Groups for persons who have offended are valuable places for support and confrontation. Sexual abuse is such a secretive and private offense. Therefore, it is powerful and effective to disclose and discuss it in a safe group setting. In working with groups of men, I am constantly amazed at the ability of individuals to see through the rationalizations of others when at times they have not seen their own rationalizing as clearly.

Many men describe themselves as loners and say they cannot talk in a group setting. Perhaps that is why group involvement is pivotal in restoring their sense of connection with themselves and with others who have offended. With such a framework, the men can go on to establish connections with the broader community.

> *Rob:* I believe strongly in group therapy, where the members can be challenged. In my experience, often a therapist in one-to-one therapy does not challenge as effectively as another sex offender would.

Individual counseling on a sustained basis is important to complement group involvement for James. In counseling, James can build his self-esteem and begin to explore his own past hurts. As he acquires these tools, he is better able to accept responsibility for the acts he committed and their implications for Julie and others.

Frequently group members have told me that something in the group session triggered an issue for them that they dealt with more fully in individual counseling. On other occasions, group members develop new patterns of communicating in individual sessions and take them to the group sessions as forms of "practice laboratory."

As James moves through a process of healing in a variety of settings, he and his community must persistently attend to the abuse of power that is so central to sexual abuse. He also needs checkpoints where he receives honest reviews and response.[2]

Frequently men who abuse see themselves as inept and totally lacking self-esteem. With this self-image, they often have difficulty imagining themselves as being overpowering, even to a child. They discount their physical stature and the parental authority they carry and thus do not understand their true relationship to their victims. They may make the mistake of counting the abuse as a voluntary sexual relationship between peers.

> *Jimmy:* From my perspective, most offenders have low self-esteem and are loners. Because they are loners, the outside world does not appeal to them, so they look to those who are close to them for affection and support. Often they take it from a daughter or stepdaughter, as I did in my situation.

Restoration for Julie

As the victim of the wrongful acts by her stepfather, James, Julie needed first to be believed. This seems like an obvious and simple statement. However, often the listener does not clearly state that he or she believes the victim. The victim wonders how others are interpreting what she has told them. This is especially true if sexual abuse is not disclosed until many years after its occurrence.

Julie needs to have her community listen to her with compassion and understanding and allow her to make choices regarding her future relationship with the person who harmed her. Family and community members could easily pressure her to renew her relationship with James, in spite of the possibly harmful side effects for her. The community must show sensitivity and respect for her wishes. Otherwise, her hurts could get buried deeper and deeper inside her subconscious mind.

Julie needs to hear a consistent message from everyone who relates to her and is aware of the offense: "What happened is not your fault." It can be difficult for a young person to truly believe this, even if she has heard it stated many times. Rebecca, a member of the Book Reference Group, says she frequently heard people say that it was not the victim's fault. She accepted that other victims were not to blame for what happened, but she still held *herself* personally responsible in her own situation.

When no one deals with the abuse until long after its occurrence, the victim experiences additional layers of pain in that period. The victim has a deep sense of betrayal but is forced to act as if nothing were amiss. Victims invest differing amounts of psychic energy in managing this duality.

Sometimes victims develop elaborate coping systems. They learn ways to separate or dissociate themselves from the pain of sexual abuse. Over time, this dissociation may be expressed in a variety of personalities, called multiple personality disorder. Such a reaction shows the effort a child must make to maintain an outer sense of normalcy. Most survivors struggle with some degree of dissociation or being split off from their bodies.

Individual and group counseling help victims validate their hurt and assist them in the journey toward wholeness. Many women feel most comfortable receiving counseling from a female, especially if their abuser was male. For adult male victims, it may be more difficult to find a counselor of either sex with whom they feel safe. So few male victims feel safe in acknowledging that sexual abuse is an issue, since society expects males to be stoic. The male victim's ability to trust a particular counselor may also be affected by the gender of his offender.

Support groups are important because they validate the survivors' hurt and pain. In addition, the groups provide an opportunity to observe how others have coped and to gain support in what has often been a lonely journey.

Sometimes people in Julie's situation do not want to face the issues. If that is the situation, it is important for the community to avoid labeling or blaming her or him for that stance. Instead, the community should continue to provide support and opportunities to work on the issues when the victim is ready to do so. It is counterproductive to force a victim to take counseling or attend a group.

Rachel's Dilemma

Rachel has two conflicting roles. As the wife of James and the mother of Julie, she may feel torn by her dual connection to these two who are separated by such a wide chasm. How can she resolve the tension between protecting her daughter and supporting her spouse? In the past, mothers were often accused of having subconsciously manipulated and coached their daughters into sexual involvement with the husband. That is generally not true.

Frequently these mothers carry a heavy load of duties inside and outside the home; then they are blamed for their absence from the home. In other situations, a child discloses the abuse to the mother, who then tries to get her husband to stop it. Years later she learns that the sexualized activity continued despite her intervention.

Mothers need support to gain a perspective when their world has been shattered by a disclosure of sexual abuse. Unfortunately, they have frequently been handed guilt and blame, indirectly or openly. They need understanding and compassion.

Frequently mothers find help in a group where they can talk with others at varying stages in their journey. Shame still surrounds the issue. Mothers find healing when they have a supportive and affirming place where they can talk about the family shame. They often must make major decisions about the future of the family, and it is important for them to have the necessary individual and group supports.

Often the opinions of the extended family increase the tension. For example, a mother wants to work toward reuniting the family, but extended family members are opposed. Those who support such mothers can encourage them and their family members to dialogue about their differences respectfully and openly.[3]

Greg's Questioning

Greg was not a victim of sexual abuse, but his whole life changed drastically with the disclosure of sexual abuse in his family. As stated earlier, if he had a positive relationship with James, he will likely resent his sister, Julie, and see her as the cause of his problems. He may pursue counseling as part of a family group with his mother and sister or by himself.

However, frequently individuals in Greg's position respond with anger and/or withdrawal. If other family members support open and orderly processing of the abuse, then Greg will likely not react so negatively. But if other family members express much anger and unrest about the intrusion by outside agencies, it will be more difficult for him to come to terms with what has occurred.

When sexual abuse is disclosed in a family, the intense emotional reactions are overwhelming for family members. It takes considerable time and effort to work on the issues. At the same time, it is necessary and healthy to carry on with "business as usual." For Greg, it will likely be more important for him to participate on his favorite sports team than to attend counseling sessions. His feelings and perceptions as a "nonaffected member" need to be taken into account.

Yet Greg needs to know that he can talk about the issues

when he is ready and that his feelings of anger, hurt, and betrayal will be respected, not ignored. Although he was not a direct victim, he may still be overwhelmed by the impact of the disclosure of the abuse.

Pastor Cooke's Needs and Responsibilities

Pastor Cooke may find his position is lonely and isolating. How does he balance his responsibilities as a confidential counselor with his role as congregational leader? Others may think he is protecting or shielding an offender. Nevertheless, he is a pastor to all the members of his church. It is challenging for him to function directly and openly in a way that does not compromise his position and role, while maintaining appropriate confidentiality.

The pastor also needs to explore and resolve his own doubts about this family situation. It is usually essential that he link with other members of the congregation in responding to the situation. Ideally, he will consult with and gain support from someone outside his congregation to help him sort out his various roles and responses.[4]

Conclusion

We have considered the perspectives of all those affected by the abuse. We support them in their efforts to work toward a resolution. However, working toward a resolution of the *issues* does not automatically mean that the family will be reunited. In some cases, the family unit will be restored. However, in many situations, the fractured and broken relationships cannot be mended to insure full trust and safety for all family members.

Even if the family is not reunited, that does not necessarily mean failure. Individual members may have experienced much growth and healing. Rather than sending messages of judgment and failure, the community can respect the way these family members have healed from the deep pain and anguish of sexual abuse.

6

Abuse by a Church Leader

The Good News Christian Church (GNCC) was pleased to finally have a new pastor after lay leaders had shared the duties for more than a year. Pastor John Errin seemed to possess all the qualities the congregation had identified in their pastoral search profile. The way they found him also seemed providential. The chair of the church board, Andrew Stephens, heard Pastor Errin preach the youth sermon at a conference. Andrew felt his fervor was just what GNCC needed.

All the reference checks emphasized Errin's abilities as a preacher and worship leader. When the church board considered the matter, many said Pastor Errin was an "answer to prayer." The group sensed a clear indication of God's leading. They approached Pastor Errin. After "prayerful consideration," he agreed to move his family halfway across the continent to take on this assignment.

There was great rejoicing at Good News. Everyone realized how draining it had been for them to fill all the pastoral roles. They vowed to be supportive of the new pastor and to better appreciate the difficulties and stresses of his position.

Pastor Errin came with high enthusiasm. After three years the congregation was, for the most part, pleased with his performance. In a review, members noted his inspiring sermons and the increase in Sunday morning worship attendance.

Because of Pastor Errin's obvious success as a leader, the allegation of pastoral sexual misconduct came as quite a shock. No one on the church board was sure just when the concerns were raised and who was first aware of them. There was a rumor that one board member had quietly "dealt with the matter" without informing the others. Esther Beynon's "anonymous" letter blew things wide open.

A member of the church board directly asked Esther, the junior Sunday school superintendent, about the rumors. She replied that the pastor had been making sexually inappropriate gestures toward her for sixteen months or more. She then made her comments public in an unsigned open letter to the congregation. In a few days everyone in the congregation knew who wrote the letter. She resigned from the congregation a week later, largely because of the responses she had received: strong and volatile criticism from some and silent rejection from others.

Several years later, Esther described what happened:

> I was fairly new at that church but had gotten quite involved in the program, and it felt rewarding. I was having some difficulty coping with a death in my family. After checking with counseling agencies that had long waiting lists, I decided to get counseling from the pastor.
>
> After about four sessions, I felt I was getting a handle on things and would not need to return. At that session, Pastor Errin told me, "The root of your problem is sexual." He insisted, "I'm just the one to help you feel good about your body." I tried to say no, in as polite a fashion as I could. He missed no opportunity to tell me what he thought my sexual problems were and how he could help. He would corner me in the workroom by the photocopier or try to rub my breasts as he went by.
>
> Once when a group of us were doing a church-related service project, he decided to go out and get a treat for everyone. He came back with Popsicles. Later that night, he called me at home and said he chose Popsicles because he wanted to see me licking something that was long and hard.
>
> My friend suggested that I speak to an elder on the church board. That elder responded, "This is hard to believe

. . . . Our pastor is a warm and caring person. He hugs everyone; that's just his way. Think how an accusation like this would hurt his family and all his friends . . . . Look at all the good he is doing at GNCC and in the community." He assured me he would keep the matter confidential and would discuss my concerns directly with the pastor.

During the next few months, nothing changed in the pastor's comments and activities toward me. When I called the elder again and asked if he had spoken to the pastor, he said no, that the right opportunity hadn't come up yet.

Several weeks later I received an angry call from the pastor, wanting to know why I had talked to the elder. He accused me of lying and seemed pretty sure the church board member would not believe me. Later a friend of mine told me that at a committee meeting, the pastor had described me as a person who "has problems" and "has a lot of difficulty with honesty."

I then wrote an anonymous letter to the congregation, detailing his inappropriate sexual conduct. Then, because of people's negative reaction to me, I began to distance myself from the church and then resigned as Sunday school superintendent. That was difficult for me because I didn't know many people outside the church, and church was important for me. Nevertheless, I cut back the commitments I had made so I wouldn't need to be around him.

I have since married and moved to another city. He still calls me on occasion, and I am polite and hang up as quickly as possible without allowing him to start any conversation. I no longer attend a church of this denomination, but I know friends at his former church still hold him in high regard.

He continues to work for a church-related agency that requires many volunteers. It is not surprising to me that the turnover rate for volunteers is quite high. He is charming and youthful looking and has many connections within the church and business community.

This experience has made me very cynical about leaders and pastors in particular. When I read so much debate about abortion and homosexuality in the church periodicals, I get very angry. Perhaps we should focus on ourselves, our basic lives, and how we conduct ourselves every day with the people we meet. No one wants to admit that clergy sexual abuse is an ugly problem that isn't going away.[1]

The Good News Christian Church handled their clergy misconduct case poorly. Much damage was done. Esther and others were left to recover as well as they could. The pastor received no messages challenging his abusive behaviors or moving him toward healing. Such troubling responses by a church are common. However, now we know more helpful ways to respond to the trauma of sexual abuse. We must have the courage and compassion to use those effective ways!

Handling Sexual Abuse by a Church Leader

We have considered a range of repercussions that follow sexual abuse. In this chapter we explore another layer in this complex issue, as we examine the additional ripples or waves of effect that appear when a church leader, with authority and power, betrays the trust of someone in his or her care.

Sometimes church members conclude that the victim(s) misunderstood the situation or somehow arranged for it to happen. That cannot immediately be ruled out as impossible. However, often in "victim blaming," the victim is held most responsible for the community's mistrust and confusion.

The victims of clergy sexual misconduct describe effects similar to those who suffer other forms of sexual abuse. They frequently feel encroachment, intrusion, and a lack of personal safety, even when there have been no direct threats. In some cases, the church leader has made direct threats to ruin the victim's reputation or physically hurt her, and this further violates her sense of safety.

The impact of sexual abuse, while most directly affecting the victim, also touches others. The person who has been assaulted is surrounded by others, possibly a spouse, siblings, family members, and a broader network of people who may be somewhat aware of the abuse and who are affected by it. Especially in the case of a church leader committing sexual abuse, the atmosphere of a congregation tends to become highly polarized, with people taking sides.

A pastor's spouse can be in an awkward position. If the spouse has incomplete information about the alleged actions of the partner, she cannot assess the problem and may not even be open to receiving knowledge. A spouse experiences tension in trying to determine the correct level of loyalty for her partner. If there is clearly a problem, the spouse may still struggle, particularly if the behavior is not acknowledged by the church leader or is minimized or trivialized.

Sometimes people become pastors because they hope to overcome particular tendencies in themselves and believe their leadership role will assist in their own healing.

> *Iris:* I know about a minister who felt powerless with regard to his sexual habits. He couldn't talk about his problem, and he could not stop his behavior. So he decided to become a minister. He thought if he became a minister, then he would be able to control his habit. He was thinking about power and decided to address his powerlessness by being a minister. But it didn't work.

A call to ministry is a significant commitment. For most, it is an honorable undertaking. Before we trust someone with so vital a role, it is important for church or conference officials to take precautions to avoid situations such as the one described above.

> *Jimmy:* I understand what you mean about power. I had power, and I abused it with my stepdaughter. But I also know that if I had tried the same thing with an adult female, it would not have worked. So I know that you go to the weakest person. In my case, it was a child; with the pastor, it was a vulnerable person he had power over in the church.

Betrayal of Pastoral Role

The pastor is a responsible individual and a trusted church leader. In that position, he has a professional obligation to people under his pastoral care. People pursue counseling and support when they are vulnerable and fragile. They seek spiritual direction from leaders they believe they can trust to guide them toward healing. If that vulnerability is exploited for personal gain or sexual purposes, the response to the exploitation must acknowledge this added dimension of harm and betrayal.

Church members often see the pastor as a God-substitute, one to be trusted with the most personal details. The thought that the pastor might abuse that vulnerability and use the parishioner for his own sexual fulfillment is difficult to reconcile with the image of a pastor and a God-representative. If church members have had a positive pastor-parish relationship, previously free from any concerns now being alleged, they will have a struggle to believe the victim's statement. Each person must recognize that while he or she may have experienced the pastor as offering compassionate support and caring, others genuinely have felt harmed by his actions that crossed sexual boundaries.

It is important to deal with the many facets of the wrongdoer as well. Often there is an impression left that everything the pastor has achieved is undermined by the abuse and has no value. Such is not necessarily the case. Some people seem totally obsessed with their sexual addiction,[2] and it clouds their every activity. Many individuals struggle with their own demons, which they sometimes overcome. However, in other situations, they succumb in a manner that harms others.

Sometimes church members make an extra effort to convince others in a congregation that a pastoral leader could be capable of uncharacteristic acts. They emphasize the harm that has been done and speak in a manner that brings on counterargument and a defensive reaction. "Non-offended" parishioners will be more willing to believe the allegations if they can hold onto their experiences with the pastor as a positive and spiritual influence. The damage is not minimized or downplayed; it is added to the other perceptions of the pastor.

Frequently persons abused by a pastor blame themselves, especially if they hear that message from others in the congregation.

Iris: In my situation, where I went to talk to a pastor-counselor about past sexual abuse and he sexualized the relationship, I shouldered at least half of the responsibility and named it adultery on my part. An article by Pamela Cooper White in *Christian Century* [Feb. 20, 1991] helped me clarify the issue. She stated, "Even when adultery is involved, unfaithfulness is not the primary issue."

I found her article validating me when people around me were at various levels of denial. I also believed for a long time that I was responsible, that if I had been more mature, smarter, and less vulnerable, I would have been able to avoid the problem. I lived with the pain of shouldering that responsibility for a long time.

Dealing with Sexual Misconduct Openly

When a pastor is trusted by the church community and abuses someone, the whole church body is hurt. Thus the whole community needs to be involved in recognizing that wrong and working for healing.

Some church leaders want to handle matters quickly and quietly. Secrecy usually means that only a few people know. The truth does not reach everyone potentially affected by the allegation, including the congregation as a whole. This is the most common mistake that leads to difficulty in handling allegations of clergy abuse. Processing the matter privately may hide the issue for a time, but it will no doubt resurface.

Rumors and gossip will spread information and misinformation. When more complaints surface from others in the congregation, the reaction is predictably one of disbelief and blame. "You're probably just making it up because of all the attention Esther got when she raised the issue initially," one complainant was told. But without a clear process for dealing with concerns, it is unfair to blame the victim for not raising the issue at the "proper" time.

Compare this with a situation of child sexual abuse. Someone reports to the child protection authorities that a man has sexualized a relationship with his daughter. It is standard practice to interview other children in the family, male and female, to determine if the father has sexually abused other family members dependent on him for care and nurture. The concern about other children being at risk or harmed overrides the individual's right to privacy and confidentiality. It is wise and important to uncover as much of the issue as possible at the time of the allegations.

When I use this example and apply it to pastoral sexual abuse, I have been told that it is humiliating and mean-spirited to discuss the pastor's misconduct openly in the congregation. However, we must consider the confidential nature of the work of pastors and other professionals and the guilt that their victims feel. We don't know whether others have been harmed. When we open up the investigation of the allegations, we provide a safe place for other victims to tell their experiences. We don't presume that further instances have occurred. We open up communication because we know that pastors who offend tend to minimize or downplay any other instances. They probably will not identify other possible victims.

Investigative Process

Churches often wrestle with whether to involve anyone outside their community in checking out the allegations. Their reluctance is understandable. Yet as indicated earlier, to dispose of the matter quietly and privately is like placing a Band-Aid on a festering sore. Eventually the issue is raised again in some other format.

Investigation must be done by a body that is external and impartial enough to gain the confidence of various groups affected by the allegation. That body will provide due process and fairness. Frequently concerns are raised in veiled or indirect fashion. For this reason, the investigators need to have direct contact with persons who are raising allegations. The investigators then can confirm the substance of the complaint(s) *before* hearing directly from the person accused of wrongdoing.

The meetings with the accusers must be private, with the accusers accompanied by their support persons. It is essential that there be broader sharing of the findings in a summary written form after the investigation is completed. Otherwise, inaccurate versions and interpretations will spread through the church community and will probably undermine efforts to bring closure to the issue.

The recommendations of the investigators can go beyond the specifics of the allegations to provide directions and suggestions for the church as a body. Such guidance can shape the church's future policies and procedures. It can help to ensure a clear and specific understanding of roles and relationships to minimize the probability of further abuse.

Is Full Restoration Possible?

A restorative justice approach means that those persons affected should have an opportunity for involvement in dealing with the wrongs. When the allegations are valid, it is important to seek healing for all those affected. In restoration, we do not dismiss the consequences of a wrong; we do not sidestep or ignore the effects of abuse.

Often there are differing opinions about what is a sound basis for restoration of a wrongdoer. Given the dilemma, church officials tend to delay and avoid facing issues directly and honestly. This can lead to reactions like the following from Rob:

> *Rob:* It's so easy to get disillusioned with the church. I was a part of the church when I offended; I was also there earlier when I was a victim of sexual abuse. I have stuck with the church throughout, but right now I am quite disillusioned. Now I am living in a new community, so I went to the church a few months ago and shared with the pastor. I told him about my situation, what happened, and what I've been through.
>
> When we came to talking about where I want to go with further church involvement, I got discouraging comments from him about going in that direction. I hate being discouraged. The pastor made discouraging comments about one of my work-related goals. Right now I am working at a minimum-wage job, which is not a bad job. But I went to college for a reason, and now I cannot use the education I have because I offended. I take responsibility for my offending. I know I did it. But is there a point in my life

where I can move on? Does everybody have to hold me back? This is why I am really disillusioned with the church. They do not seem to be able to move beyond the offending.

While Rob's offending was not in a church setting, it did involve sexual abuse of a person in his care. Iris responded:

Iris: Rob spoke about wanting to move on in the church. My reaction is that it takes considerable time to rebuild trust after coming through such an experience. Five years is really a fairly short time. I might not be ready to give you unlimited opportunity to serve in the church. If an offender wishes to serve again in the church while he is recovering, it is essential to have someone to mentor him, someone for him to be accountable to; in addition, he needs to have a solid support system. Future service opportunities can then be evaluated in the light of this recovery process.

As mentioned earlier, sometimes disciplinary bodies choose to delay and avoid making a decision. That leaves the person who has offended in limbo, without a clear process or healing journey to pursue. At the same time, there are consequences for one's actions. Therefore, some future career goals may not be appropriate. Things can never be what they were before; safety for the vulnerable must be the primary consideration.

Iris: What is the answer when a minister has sexually offended? Will he ever be reinstated as a minister? Theoretically, the church should not rule it out. But I wonder how practical it really is for many offenders to be ministers again.

Marie M. Fortune explores this issue and emphasizes the need to protect vulnerable people:

Ministry is a privilege, not a right. A clergy person forfeits this privilege when he/she betrays the trust of a congregant. It is the responsibility of the denominational body to do everything it can to insure that an abusive clergy person does not have access to vulnerable people in the future. (This is probably also the point of greatest potential liability for the denominational body.)[3]

Corporate Healing

The impact of sexual abuse by a church leader goes beyond the victim of the particular violation. Every member of the congregation is affected somewhat by the pastor's action and the process of coping with it. A church community needs corporate healing as well as an investigative team to guide the process. Most churches have found that clergy misconduct brings to the surface other internal conflicts that were in the church and typically are present in every congregation, to some degree.

In a congregation that dealt with the aftermath of sexual abuse by congregational leader, one member stated,

> When there is confession of sexual abuse, the reactions are not just about the offender and the victim. I think anything that violates boundaries this seriously brings out each person's sexuality. How we respond to the offender may say as much about ourselves, what we need to hide, what we need to avenge, as it does about the offender.
>
> The most profound effect for our group was all kinds of mistrust and attempts to find solutions. Battles emerged on other issues totally unrelated to the situation because the basic question that emerges is: "If you can't trust your elder and minister, whom can you trust?"[4]

The diversity of opinion in any church board following a disclosure is probably similar to the range of opinion in the congregation. It is not a matter of simply giving the "correct" information and moving on. Matters such as this trigger many personal and interpersonal issues for congregants. These issues require time and a predictable process that points to some resolution and healing.

There is hope and reason for optimism that churches can change and can face the unthinkable. Consider this comment from a member of one church, almost five years after clergy misconduct was revealed in the congregation:

> As a church, it is only in the past six months that we have begun to emerge out of our "stuckness." I cannot say how many of our struggles have been connected directly with the pastor. There were other things brewing and some changes needed, but the disclosure certainly opened up all kinds of bad stuff.
>
> Our church is half the size that it was, but a new spirit of hope and excitement is emerging among us. The long and painful hours of meeting with an outside facilitator were, I think, integral to getting out of the bondage. One key was the prayers of many, especially a special prayer night by a sister congregation.[5]

Because of the deep hurts of so many people, we need to urgently work for prevention of sexual abuse so that in the future people won't have to struggle through such tragedies.

Guidelines for Handling Clergy Misconduct

A myriad of challenges face those who are trying to respond to sexual abuse by church leaders. How do individuals and governing bodies find their way through the maze of broken relationships, intense emotions, grieving souls, and overwhelming issues? Each situation is unique. However, other peoples' experiences are useful.

The broader context helps to provide perspective and consistency. It is crucial to find appropriate expertise. Because of the multilayered dynamics, persons with relevant experience and training are required. In addition, the following questions are provided to assist in dealing with specific situations:

1. Considering Legal Issues

Leaders who handle church leader abuse must be aware of possible civil and criminal liabilities. It is important to respect the accused's rights to a fair procedure.

A. Has there been appropriate *documentation* of the complaint? Usually the complainant submits a written statement, though the identity of the writer may not be shared, at least not initially. This allows investigators to proceed with the complaint in a systematic and defensible manner. It should never be used as a way to discount or undermine the complainant.

B. Is there a *procedure* in place by the governing body responsible, and is it being adhered to? If there is no procedure in place, it is immensely complicated to try to design one while at the same time implementing it in a specific case. If a procedure is in place, it should be followed. If it is not followed, difficulties could arise later, if there is an appeal or counteraction by one of the parties. It is important not only to have a procedure but also to have it updated in accordance with current practice.

C. Have child protection *authorities* been *notified?* Even where the current complainant(s) are adult(s), it is important to consult with child protection to insure that there are not other related matters. For example, there could be an earlier complaint concerning the accused that only child protection agencies are aware of. Sometimes making an initial call anonymously can be helpful in gaining necessary information.

In discussing legal issues, the focus tends to be largely on the person accused and protecting her/his rights. On many occasions, complainant(s) report that they felt left out of the process. If leaders are sensitive to this issue and openly work on it with the complainant(s), there will be less misunderstanding.

2. Providing Safety

The public disclosure of boundary crossing by a church leader almost always causes considerable trauma for the complainant(s). It is important to give advance thought to this vulnerability and fear and to provide information on how the process will unfold. In addition, those in charge should tend to practical applications such as church seating arrangements, or asking the accused not to currently attend the worship services. This will assist in removing some of the uncertainty.

A. Is the *complainant consulted* on what situations are of greatest concern?

B. Is attention given to *safety concerns* for other family members of the complainant(s)?

C. Is attention given to *safety concerns* for other family members of the person accused?

D. Are avenues provided for other members of the *church community* to confidentially discuss the disclosure and the implications for them?

E. Do *congregational* prayers, rituals, and symbols give *recognition* to the significant matter being handled?

3. Caring for the Needs of All Persons Affected

The ripple or wave effect of an event as traumatic as the betrayal of trust by a church leader has far-reaching impacts within a congregation. People need time and appropriate settings to process what is happening and work toward resolution. Information, support, and time are essential elements in the healing process for all persons affected.

A. *Is* a plan in place to provide *pastoral care* for all persons affected?

B. Do persons in leadership positions provide *support and information* in a way that does not further polarize people already divided by the issue?

C. Are *spiritual and pastoral issues* of all persons addressed?

D. Is *genuine repentance* encouraged and nurtured?

4. Making the Process Clear and Open Enough

In matters of boundary violation by a church leader, there is a tendency to minimize and avoid. As a general principle, all persons affected should have information about what has occurred.

A. Has a concise *plan* been formulated and shared? Has there been *outside consultation* on the plan and its implementation?

B. Are persons involved in dealing with the issues *aware of the complications* that can occur if there are dual roles? For example, a designated agency staff person might accept a statement from a complainant and provide empathetic support in the course of the disclosure. That staff person, perceived as supportive to the complainant, may subsequently have responsibilities towards a co-worker who is the accused. To avoid this con-fusion, the staff person could empathically take the com-plainant's information with a support person (or advocate) present. By so doing, the staff person attempts to avoid being in a dual role.

C. Do the individuals implementing the process recognize both the *dynamics* present when power is abused and the need to maintain a sense of *fairness?* Sometimes in a stated desire to be "fair," investigators dismiss factors that make one party vul-nerable to the sexual advances of the other. Differences in age, sex, race, sexual orientation, or economic status can dramatical-ly impact whether a complainant is believed. The investigating body must have an awareness of these implications and take them into account in its deliberations. At the same time, the fairness of the process must be maintained. Frequently a back-lash occurs when people minimize the wrong because they feel sympathy for the way someone accused has been treated or mistreated. This is counterproductive to the process.

D. Is there a plan for *accountability and closure?* In addition to the treatment and support that the accused may require, there is a need for a process that follows the progress of the wrongdoer in her/his healing journey. In *Restoring the Fallen: A Team Approach to Caring, Confronting and Reconciling,* the authors provide a systematic and comprehensive model to pro-vide for accountability in professional and spiritual dimensions.[6]

The issues surrounding clergy abuse are not primarily the-oretical, psychological, or theological. They are personal, spiri-tual, and relational. The accountability group must invite, entice, and encourage the abuser to face these issues and work on them. Thus they may break through the abuser's veneer of denial and minimization.

Such a process is typically undertaken as part of an institu-tional credentialing process, where the affected party relin-quishes ordination or another professional license. The account-ability group's ability to follow through on such an approach may be limited. However, any authentic restorative process depends on the wrongdoer's openness to being influenced by and accepting direction from trusted persons. Hence, we hope other avenues of corrective discipline can be found. If the accountability group is not able to influence the wrongdoer through personal relationships or removal of credentials, it is still important to use effective ways of informing potential future victims about the danger.

7

How Does Healing Come?

It is not the wound that determines the quality of your life, it's what you do with the wound—how you hold it, carry it, dance with it, or bury yourself under it. No one knows where dreams are born and what gives people the grit to follow them. Lucille Ball's father died when she was four. Her mother remarried but sent Lucille to live with relatives. They put a dog collar around her neck and tied her to a tree in the backyard to keep her from wandering. While her body was tied down, her mind wandered. She created a friend called Sassafras, who comforted her and told her that she would be a famous movie star.

Life is what happens as you live with the wounds. Life is not a matter of getting the wounds out of the way so that you can finally live. Wounds are never permanently erased. We are fragile beings, and some days we break all over again. Being an abandoned person changes from year to year, depending upon how conscious you are about that piece of yourself. How much are you willing to risk? How patient are you willing to be? How much mercy can you give to that part of you that is forever afraid of being left? The way you work with your fear of abandonment shapes the curves and colors of your life the way the river shapes a canyon wall.

Healing is about opening our hearts, not closing them. It is about softening the places in us that won't let love in.

Healing is a process. It is about rocking back and forth between the abuse of the past and the fullness of the present, and being in the present more and more of the time. It is the rocking that creates the healing, not staying in one place or another. The purpose of healing is to be awake and to live while you are still alive instead of dying while you are still alive. Healing is about being broken and whole at the same time.[1]

The healing journey is a winding trail, not a superhighway. It is a journey traveled by each of us—victims, those who have offended, family members, clergy, friends, therapists. We travel, with differing degrees of urgency or concentration. What is helpful or therapeutic for one person may have the opposite impact on another. Here we listen to the perspectives of women and men on a healing journey; their voices carry the weight of this chapter.

When the Book Reference Group met to discuss healing, they identified their anxiety in broaching such a raw and sensitive topic. We began by inviting people to share one word that expressed their feelings about healing. Alexandra spoke first:

> *Alexandra:* My word is *trepidation*. It's funny because, as I said to Rebecca as we got out of the car, "I feel full of trepidation about this tonight" [the group laughed sympathetically]. I have been discouraged the past three weeks, struggling with work, thinking that I cannot do things and that I'm a failure. So looking at healing right now is scary.

Other group members agreed. Persons with direct experience in sexual abuse often voice such feelings about healing. It is a long, difficult, and sometimes frightening journey.

In this chapter we primarily look at the healing of those who have offended, and we use the additional experience of survivors to broaden that perspective. While there may be similarities, the healing journeys of survivors and those that have offended have different origins and dynamics. As you read, consider the similarities and differences without evaluating or criticizing those healing journeys.

Motivation for Beginning

Two men who have sexually offended discuss their motivation for beginning to work for healing:

> *Gary:* If I imagined going through the rest of my life without working for recovery, it means I would live the rest of my life going through the torture of trying to stop myself from re-offending. I think that would be worse and much harder than the healing option I am undertaking.

> *Jimmy:* If you don't work at healing, then you are still liable to offend. You have to heal yourself. But it's more than just a fear that you might re-offend. I also have a desire to be made whole and become a better person. I want to become a different person. The old person isn't somebody that people want to have around. I really don't want to be that horrible person anymore.

Accountability is a term that is often used regarding those who have offended. The community's interest in accountability is in part an attempt to insure that the individual does not drift back to past patterns and behaviors.

> *Steve:* Sometimes when people are responding to an offender in terms of accountability, it could seem as if people are watching over you, checking on you. There is always the hidden question, "Is he going to re-offend?" To me, that's not necessarily bad.

The Need to Heal

Those who have offended have difficulty recognizing their need to heal. However, that is a critical first step.

> *Jimmy:* I have a lot of fear in my heart as I wonder: Can I heal? But it's not just about the offending; it's also about all the other faults I have. I have been an angry person all my life, for example. I never thought of myself in that way before. There are many things I am learning about myself on top of healing from being a "sex offender." I can see lots of other things about me that I do not like, and I wonder

how many of these I will succeed in changing.

Steve: I am learning from this group that healing of hurts takes a long time and a lot of hard work. I find that I have to be careful not to downplay or minimize that for myself. Often I would like to think I am further down the road than I am. I struggle with that because there is a part of me that wants to see light, but I am often overwhelmed by darkness that clouds over, and it is awful shady! It's like somebody pulled the blinds and blocked out the sunlight.

Jimmy: I've learned that it's a long road back, and I haven't come to the end of the road. I don't know if I ever will. I feel as if I am halfway through a tunnel, and although I am starting to feel good about myself, that other half of the tunnel seems harder to climb, for some reason. I feel like I'm getting some of my self-respect back. Previously I hated and hurt myself, and I finally realized that I cannot do that forever. It's not good for me, and it's not good for anyone else.

Iris: The topic of healing is very close to my heart. I believe that as I progress in my healing journey, I will be helping not only myself, but also other victim-survivors as well as offenders and those who are both victims and offenders. There is one thing that I think covers both hurts and the need for healing. That one thing is "the lie." It hurts to live a life of the lie, which kept me a victim for so many years. The lie needs to be exposed, and the truth needs to emerge so that both victim and offender can begin to be free and begin to heal.

Steve: My hurts were related to a lot of confusing childhood stuff. Still, it was an important step for me to be able to admit that I made a bad choice in dealing with my own hurts. It was my choice, and all other excuses would just get me all mixed up. For me, choosing a healing path is not an easy way out. It's more difficult but also more rewarding.

Framework for Seeking Offender Healing

Healing begins for those who have offended when they

(1) acknowledge what they did and (2) accept responsibility for those wrongful actions. These essential steps lead to (3) a marked change in their behavior and orientation. This will be visible to those who relate to them. Unless healing is undertaken is this context, it will be short-lived and will inevitably lead to a repeat of past patterns and re-offending. Let's look at these factors in greater detail.

1. Acknowledging the wrong

It seems obvious that the person who offended must acknowledge the wrong, but the community must be clear and direct about it. We all trend to avoid the traumatic details of sexual abuse; it is difficult to look honestly and directly at such harm. In response to external pressure, an individual may engage in treatment without truly acknowledging his abuse, for example, that his hand touched the vagina of a young girl, a specific child whom he harmed. As discussed further in chapter 12, the person who offended frequently minimizes or denies the sexual abuse.

For genuine healing to take place, the individual must openly acknowledge the abuse. Others interacting with the person must make it clear that such acknowledgment is essential to their healing journey. Some persons may say they want to heal, but they claim to have no memory of their acts. Genuine healing requires recall and acknowledgment.

2. Accepting responsibility

Taking responsibility may come gradually, perhaps with community support and prodding, but ultimately it must be a decision by the person who offended. Otherwise it does not involve the individual's own conscience and therefore does not lead to healing. Acts of sexual abuse are reprehensible. The offending person may even acknowledge this as a fact but with no feeling of remorse or personal responsibility. Fully assuming responsibility will take some time. When the individual has allowed that sense of responsibility to percolate deep within, then he may find true healing and a resulting change in behavior.[2]

3. Changing behavior and orientation

Changed behavior comes after the individual acknowledges the abuse and accepts responsibility. It is the fruit of the commitment to go in a new healing direction built on a solid foundation. It means no further violations of sexual boundaries, and it means far more. The individual will gain a greater ability to be open and honest in relationships and in sharing feelings such as anger, frustration, happiness, and pleasure. Consider the voices of those on this journey.

"What I Needed and Need for My Healing"

Those who have offended can learn much from the experiences of survivors of sexual trauma. Alexandra shares her perspective on what she needed for her healing:

> *Alexandra:* My healing has been a process of empowerment. The abuse left me feeling powerless and out of touch with what I needed and wanted. My sense of who I was and my self-esteem were damaged. I needed a lot of support to rediscover who I was, to find answers within myself, to discover my unique process of healing, and to trust my inner wisdom. I needed to be gently reminded that I had choices and that I could make good ones. I needed others to allow me to decide what I needed. I found it helpful when others offered respect and empathy for my pain and for my unique healing process.
>
> I needed to know that other survivors go through a struggle similar to mine, that I wasn't alone or crazy. At the same time, I needed to be cautious about comparing my experience with others' experiences because I have a tendency to diminish my abuse by comparing it to situations that seem worse. (For example, I would think, "She was so much younger than me," or "She was abused by her dad," etc.)
>
> I needed people to listen to me and believe me and not judge me. I found that I needed to talk about my experience a lot, to go over and over things. I just wanted to be listened to and to have someone understand and be with me while I grieved and struggled. I often felt that people's discomfort with what I was telling them made it difficult

for them to really listen. When others offered me simplistic answers (such as "get some exercise") or suggested that I should just get on with my life, I felt invalidated and unsupported. I do not want to be talked out of my needs because of someone else's discomfort with my pain.

Because I was fourteen when I was sexually abused, I carried a lot of self-hate and judgment about giving in to my abuser. Why couldn't I just keep on saying no?

I needed a lot of affirmation that the abuse wasn't my fault. I needed a lot of support to see the many ways that I had been manipulated and coerced and to realize that I was too young to be dealing with a situation like that. I needed help to get over the feelings of shame, to counteract the belief that I was "damaged goods." I needed to know that what happened was bad, but that *I* wasn't bad.

I needed to learn to feel compassion for myself about the coping mechanisms I used to survive, the depression, stuffing myself full of food, sleeping to escape. I continue to need to practice patience to learn new, healthier coping skills.

To build trust, I still need to be able to check things out with people. To ask people to clarify something they've said. To tell them how I interpreted their behavior, and to have them check out to see if I was right. I still need others to be accountable for their mistakes and to have my boundaries respected. To be free to take my time getting to know someone. Not to be pushed into doing something because it suits another person.

I still need others to set clear boundaries about how they are willing to help me rather than to have them feel obligated and then resentful. I need others to accept that I know what I need and for them to decide what they are willing to do.

I do not want to be pushed to forgive my abuser "for my own good." I don't believe that I need to confront or forgive my abuser to heal myself. If I was trying to maintain some type of relationship with him, maybe this would be different. However, he has never asked me for forgiveness or expressed regret. At this point, if that were to happen, I think I could forgive him. Once again, I still need to decide what is best for me, and not be pushed by somebody else's pat answer based on Scriptures or religious beliefs or whatever.

I do not want to hear that my abuser couldn't help what he did because he was crazy, hurting, or whatever. I feel that these comments negate or invalidate my pain and my experience. I can now look at life histories as causal factors in abuse, but I didn't want to hear about it when I was struggling to survive. I felt as if my abuser was being left off the hook. Yes, he had a rough life, but he still had no right to do what he did, and he is responsible for his behavior.

I need to remind myself of the progress I have made, and to celebrate that I have survived!

Gary Responds

Gary: As I read Alexandra's list of healing conditions, I was struck once again, as I have been many times, by the similarities in the feelings and healing process of both survivors and offenders. Let me say that I am always wary about identifying too closely. I know that offenders are the cause and survivors are the effect. I also see that both cause and effect ripple through time and society like parallel waves of sadness and pain.

Healing is healing, no matter who undertakes it. I read Alexandra's remarks as a journey toward progressive understanding and acceptance with all that that implies—understanding and acceptance of oneself and of a reality that cannot be changed. It's coming to terms with internal and external realities, with wholeness as the goal. When Alexandra speaks of feeling that she was damaged goods, I know what she means. I used that phrase myself, and I now see healing as the act of repairing damage.

When I first entered counseling four years ago, I often did not understand what I was being told, especially in the first year. But as I have learned, and practiced what I have learned, I've come to gain some perspective on my own healing process. Many of the themes Alexandra raised are identical to my own.

She used the word *empowerment* in the very first sentence. When I read that, I thought of *choices*, and so I was not at all surprised when a few sentences later I read that word. But at the beginning of my healing, I was tremendously frightened by the very concept of making choices about who I was and how I behaved. Having felt trapped for so long in a particular way of life and thought, the idea that I could make choices was foreign.

Learning that I had choices was only the first step in recognizing that choices are both a right and a responsibility that are part of my being an adult. I still have difficulty with the latter part, recognizing that I am a forty-one-year-old man who carries the responsibility of making mature, adult choices.

This eventually led me to the idea of taking care of myself. It is remarkable how often my counselors asked me in one way or another, "When are you going to start taking care of yourself?" There is so much in that small question, much of it raised by Alexandra's comments.

First, I needed to identify and acknowledge my feelings. That was and is unbelievably difficult to do, though less so as I consciously practice it. Alexandra spoke of needing to be listened to. I had been silent for so long that my decision to start talking (which I sometimes call my leap of faith into healing) resulted in an opening of floodgates of information.

That led me onto another plane. The necessity of somehow sorting out all this information required not only that I talk, but also that I begin to listen. It was only by listening to myself that I began to discover what my needs were. I soon discovered that my needs were not simply the sexual gratification I had sought through my offending. I found meditation and journaling to be important in this process of discovering my needs.

I also needed to know that I wasn't alone. I found help by entering a group for offenders and a twelve-step group. There I again discovered how useful it was to listen. In those groups, I often heard people describe feelings and needs for which I had previously not had a name. As Alexandra said, the opportunity to build trust by checking things out with people was essential, since my confidence in my own intuition was nonexistent.

Recognition of needs brought me to the establishment of boundaries, and the acceptance of other people's boundaries—another foreign concept. I learned simple things, like my right to say no. That I had a right as an adult to tell my father I did not want him to pat me on the head as if I were a child, and then not to feel guilty about it. I had a responsibility as an adult to respect the wishes of others without taking it as a personal attack.

Often, as I learn these things and speak about them to other people whom I consider "healthier," I sense their incredulity, as if they do not quite understand why I am surprised at discovering these things. The reason I am surprised is that I am realizing the hundreds of tiny cracks through which my sense of identity, self-esteem, and self-worth leaked out, and the enormous commitment needed to mend a vessel that I had allowed to fall into such disrepair.

For me, healing is a process of learning to love myself in some way, to love and care, as an adult, for all the people I have become: The hurt, needy child. The intellectually superior man and his brother, the grandiose impostor. The angry, vulgar offender and his partner, the vindictive manipulator. The compassionate man whose heart fills with wonder when he strokes a cat or watches a bird preening itself. The funny man who knows something of God's good humor in the mischief of children. The man who wants to love and who sometimes loves in spite of himself.

What an effort it is sometimes to hold them all together, listen to them, to attend to them, because as Arthur Miller says, "Attention must be paid."

From this, I gain respect for anyone in recovery, and survivors in particular, who did not ask for this opportunity. I understand some of the pain of having to sort through the mess.

Healing-recovery-therapy has been described to me as a spiral in which I always confront the same issues but at different levels of understanding. As a last word, I would like to deal with the issue of forgiveness. First, I must consider self-forgiveness. How do I undertake the massive commitment of really taking care of myself unless I forgive the errors of my past, present, and future? And unless I truly believe that I am worthy of such a commitment? I used to say, "God forgives, but I don't," but I think now I understand the complete impossibility of that, and the incredible arrogance of the idea. I must forgive God for being God, and myself for being human.

That is hard. Ultimately, it's probably the reason why my recovery doesn't shoot up into the stratosphere and render me immediately perfect. Forgiving myself for stupidity, for willful destructiveness, for fear, for weakness and lethargy—it is really, really hard.

Forgiving others is almost as hard because the hurting voice inside cries, "It's not fair, it's not fair."

Then I look at myself, and see how much I crave the forgiveness of those I have offended, and what it means to me that I may never receive it. Slowly I come around to the idea of acceptance—accepting who I am today; accepting responsibility for who I will be tomorrow; accepting those who have hurt me, intentionally or not, knowing that I choose my response; accepting the rejection of those I have hurt with the knowledge that I am willing to make what amends I can; accepting the commitment to heal.

These things occur at a slow, often agonizing pace, and not necessarily in order. But I look back and see that they do occur.

Taking Stock of the Healing Journey

Frequently persons measure their healing progress as if it were a school report card or a linear graph; they want to see systematic, steady progress. In reality, healing rarely takes that predictable a pattern. If individuals have such an expectation, they will likely engage in extensive, destructive self-doubt and feel like a failure.

Jimmy: When I was sitting in jail, I used to think of the people I know, and I'd wish I was them. I used to wish I was so-and-so, because he didn't do it. He is a good person, and I am a rotten person. I used to wish I was a cat or a dog and could stick to a simple life of eating, drinking, and sleeping. But we just have to work on ourselves.

Gary: Four years ago I didn't think I had issues. I now know I have issues to work on, and I imagine solving them, closing them up, and then they are gone. But that has never happened to me. The issues I have just seem to keep coming back.

It's more like a spiral. I find I'm always working with the same issues, but on a different level. In one way, it's pretty discouraging, but on the other hand, if I feel like I'm healing, then at least I'm dealing with it on some level. Maybe it is a step up.

I've always been amazed that I'm afraid of failure and success simultaneously. I know this comes from my relationship with my father. He will build me up while putting me down—put me down while building me up. I told my parents I wasn't going to see them until I could face my father on an adult level. But I didn't stick to that plan. I find when I go back, I respond to him like I always did. Boy, I hate that!

So after the last visit, I tried to sort it out by writing. It's like a letter to him that I haven't sent.

I wrote, "I keep hearing you say these things. It sounds like you're saying, 'What is the matter with you? You're not good enough.' I don't need to hear those kinds of blaming statements from you because I have enough of my own voices inside of me that tell me that every day."

For me, writing down those confusing and critical messages has been an important part of my healing. It'll be another big step when I am able to share it with my father.

Jimmy: Sometimes when I'm trying to deal with my issues and problems, I feel like I don't deserve to be better. Sometimes I feel I don't deserve to be happy.

Steve: For me to get out of a negative spiral, I try to get involved with other groups, mainly church groups. It's a way of gaining more self-worth. The last two weeks I spent doing maintenance work at a Christian rehab center. It was volunteer work, but I felt that I still had something to offer, that I was able to make a difference.

I look at it spiritually. God still does have a plan for my life. Sometimes it's difficult to see, but time and time again, it keeps cropping up. Sometimes when I am home all by myself, and there's not that much of a home now, the old guilt thoughts come back, and I can feel quite down on myself.

Things didn't work out as smoothly as I would have

liked. But then I wonder, "Am I being selfish and self-centered?" I think so, lots of times.

Religious Aspects of Healing

At various points in this book we have referred to the difficulties that persons recovering from sexual abuse experienced in their churches. While there are exceptions, too frequently the church community has hindered individuals from healing. Chapter 10 suggests ways the church can be helpful. When the person has not had broader church support and validation, she or he may find solace in individual faith and commitment.

Iris: My faith has sustained me through thick and thin. The love of God has nurtured me, even though I couldn't always sense God's presence. I believed God's love in spite of not always being able to see or feel it. I have had to deepen my faith in a way that I never dreamed possible. In order to continue my life of faith, I had to cry out, "My God, my God, why have you forsaken me?" I cried until there was no crying left. I know now that deep within the godless despair of sexual abuse, God was right there, suffering with me.

A woman, who discovered years later that her husband had sexually abused her nieces, writes, "I am grateful for a personal relationship with God, who gives me strength, wisdom, joy, tears, love, peace, anger, rest, and restlessness."[3]

Rob: I was a minister at one time, and that is a significant part of my identity. As I grow in my own healing, I have come to understand more deeply the meaning of some religious statements that people make quite glibly. It isn't just a matter of saying that I am going to accept Christ as my Savior, and he is going to forgive me, and that's that. There is much more to it.

How Is Healing Different Because of Abuse?

Persons affected by sexual abuse wonder how their lives would be different if not for the dramatic impact of the sexual abuse.

Alexandra: Sometimes I struggle within myself. I give myself a rough time and try to figure out why I'm like this. I have a lot of self-doubt. Am I really this way because of the sexual abuse in my life, or is this just the way I am? It's interesting to hear from people who don't identify themselves as survivors of sexual abuse, but who also struggle with issues of low self-esteem or depression or anger. One thing I can always directly link to my abuse experience is the sense of utter powerlessness that I sometimes have. I truly believe that is a learned experience.

Steve: When I first went to a counselor after the disclosure of offenses, I was in a deep pit of despair. I said, "What's normal?" At that point, I just wanted to get off the world and leave everything behind. In that respect, it was helpful for me to come to terms with what had happened, and that those extreme feelings I was having were okay. If I was feeling down and out the day that I visited the counselor, that was okay because he had also had down-and-out days sometimes, maybe not as extreme.

For me, that was helpful in encouraging me to open up and say, "I can trust this person because he goes through things, too. Perhaps he doesn't have as much baggage, but I am a person like him." I find that, despite the offenses that I committed, I am not so different from everyone else. I have needs that must be met or that I would like to have met, and my needs are quite normal. The biggest challenge for me was learning how to sort out my feelings after having grown up with a lot of mixed ideas about how I was supposed to act and supposed to feel or not feel in a particular situation.

The Group as Part of the Healing Journey

As noted in chapter 1, the Book Reference Group did not assume that the group would be a "therapy group," but we did hope that it would be "therapeutic" for the participants. As the twice-monthly meetings progressed, we noted an added dimension. The group members discussed their experience:

Iris: I'm realizing how important this group is for me. I do not have a lot of friends that I can share with about this subject; I need to widen my support base. This group is a support base for me, and that's been really nice.

Rebecca: When I do public speaking, I get negative feedback because I'm in a group like this. "How could you do that?" What I try to express is that this group is me. Whenever anyone is excluded, healing is prevented. At the same time, I want to allow other people the right to their views.

Jimmy: I've always felt that offenders had to keep their distance from survivors. It's easy to feel distant from the others' feelings so long as they are not known; they are like a shadow out there. But when survivors come to a group setting and share, you feel and understand more about them as well as about your own victim.

One survivor spoke directly to a person who had offended:

Rebecca: One of the most powerful things in my life was the time I told my story to your treatment group and you said, "It wasn't your fault." That was the first time I had heard that from someone who had offended. You said earlier tonight that you felt you hadn't contributed much to the group. I don't care if you never say another word. Your one statement to me at your group was very meaningful.

Alexandra: I like the way this group works. There have been nights when I have gone home and thought, "Yuck." And there have been nights when I have gone home and thought, "Wow, I'm glad I'm part of that group." Being in a mixed group with both offenders and survivors is really important to me as a survivor, taking the next step on my healing journey. I feel the support you are talking about. It's really important for me to see and get to know people who have offended and realize that you are people and to see you working hard at things. Your journey is very important for me.

Rebecca and Steve commented on their interactions:

Steve (to Rebecca): I feel that there has been some good stuff happening between us, Rebecca, as part of this group, and also as part of the university class presentation we did recently. The other night when we were chatting in the parking lot, you empowered me with what you said, and that felt really good afterward.

Rebecca (to the group): Steve and I had been meeting with the teacher of the university class to prepare our presentation about sexual abuse. Steve left quickly, and I thought, "Oh, he didn't really say good-bye." When I caught up with him in the parking lot, I learned that he was not sure if I felt comfortable being with him apart from structured settings. After we checked that out, we had a good conversation. It was really neat.

Group members added their own perspectives:

Iris: Sometimes it takes so much effort to gear up to check something out, and when you check it out, you find, "Oh, that was so easy!"

Gary: But with regard to victims and offenders, I think, "Once bitten, twice shy."

Rebecca: Yes, when you have the courage to check it out, you also take the risk of being told "no."

Gary: Being able to accept "no" is a most valuable thing to learn.

Avoiding Recipes for a Healing Journey

In this chapter you have heard many experiences from the lives of women and men who are courageously dealing with the impact of sexual abuse in their lives. I have not described a recipe for healing that would fit everyone. Instead, we heard individuals sharing their journeys. The most important way to assist persons in their healing journey is to offer deep respect for the ability of each person to reach deep within herself or himself and to intuitively discover what is needed to heal.

8

Unresolved Hurts from Abuse

Aaron shall lay both his hands on the head of the live goat, and confess over it all the iniquities of the people of Israel, and all their transgressions, all their sins, putting them on the head of the goat, and sending it away into the wilderness by means of someone designated for the task. The goat shall bear on itself all their iniquities to a barren region; and the goat shall be set free in the wilderness. (Lev. 16: 21-22)

This Old Testament passage explains how the people of Israel symbolically placed all their sins and transgressions on a goat that was then banished to the wilderness. The ritual was not a "once and for all" event to rid the community of its sins but was repeated each year on the Day of Atonement. Each year the community used this ritual to acknowledge and atone for their acts of wrongdoing. The term "scapegoating" comes from this ritual.[1]

We have changed much of our understanding of how transformation and redemption take place in our lives. Even so, the image of the scapegoat is relevant today. This is especially true for the issue of sexual abuse. We want so much to rid ourselves of our sexual wounds and transgressions, as individuals and corporately as a church community.

Unfortunately, our scapegoats are people—those who have offended sexually and their victims. We vainly hope that with this form of scapegoating, we can get rid of sexual abuse. However, like the Israelites, we find that wrongdoing continues: new offenders and new victims keep arising, and the cycle of futility continues. Our act of scapegoating contributes to the ongoing tragedy of sexual abuse.

We scapegoat others to deny that we all have unresolved pasts. Each of us wrestles with our desire to erase those shadowy parts of ourselves that we normally mask in daily interactions. Sexual abuse is so difficult to face because it exposes the shadow side in each of us and in our communities.

In solitude we wonder, "Do I have unresolved hurts, hidden feelings of fear, shame, and anger that sap my soul? Is my sexuality distorted and fragmented? Have I abused my power with loved ones or others?" We are haunted by the "yes" to those questions. In our discomfort and to avoid facing our own issues, we scapegoat others.

Scapegoating must end. To stop sexual abuse, each person must examine and heal his or her own hurts. In this chapter we will explore things we have in common. We all have issues that require resolution, and we have had experiences of being wronged by the willful or careless actions of others. We also need to acknowledge that we have done things that have harmed others, and we must own those actions. While my examples come from those with direct experience in sexual abuse, see how they apply to you.

Consider this exchange between members of the Book Reference Group.

Rob: It's difficult to compare ourselves with other people. I think everyone has issues to deal with, but most of the people were never forced to deal with their issues as we were.

Gary: I wonder if some people just don't want to deal with their issues.

Jimmy: Well, did we want to deal with our issues, before we offended and were confronted with what our problems were?

Rob: So, really, we are a lot like nonoffenders in that way!

Comparing Ourselves to Others

It is human nature to compare ourselves with others. Since *we* select the items to be compared, we tend to show up well. Sometimes making comparisons is a good healing strategy, and sometimes a way of avoiding the truth. Good or bad, we will always be comparing ourselves with others.

We have noted that survivors tend to compare their abuse with others to chastise themselves or minimize their trauma. Some offenders compare their actions with others to shore up their belief that their offenses were not that serious. On the other hand, sometimes comparison leads one to feel much worse than others; that results in further depression and despair.

As we've discussed before, those affected by sexual abuse often wonder how their lives would be different if they had not abused or been abused. This topic came up at various points in the Book Reference Group.

I shared that I grew up in a stable and nurturing family and did not experience childhood traumas. Yet I too have feelings of inadequacy and uncertainty about my work and life goals. How can I account for this? Like the people directly affected by sexual abuse, I sometimes scold myself for having these feelings. I compare my experiences with the traumas known by those around me. Then I think there must really be something wrong with me if I have feelings of inadequacy and no clear reason for them.

What is a helpful or useful direction to go when comparing ourselves with others? Many of us are uncomfortable with our internal reactions when we have contact with survivors or offenders of sexual abuse. In those comparisons, we do not like to see our own sexual brokenness and wounds.[2]

Can we shift our responses? Can we recognize that the pain and discomfort we experience in the presence of sexual abuse is an invitation to examine our own wounds and find healing? Without such a shift, we will continue to avoid effective action in responding to sexual abuse. We will minimize our own wounds and emphasize those of sexual abuse victims.

Recognizing Our Wounded Sexuality

According to statistics on the frequency of sexual abuse, one-fourth of females and one-sixth of males will have an unwanted sexual advance by age eighteen.[3] There are clues that these figures are underreported. Obviously, three-fourths of the women and five-sixths of the men do not report having been sexually abused.

There are no statistics on wounded and repressed sexuality, but I believe it is far more common than shown in the above statistics. Almost universally we sense that our ability to respect and enjoy our human sexuality as a wholesome gift from God has been repressed and/or deformed. Much advertising and many television shows misuse sex for sales and ratings. When we accept such things as normal, we indicate how far we are from the goal of healthy sexuality.

The impact of misdirected sexuality is not limited to the faith community. However, many church messages intended to help us avoid the pitfalls of sexuality have driven our enjoyment and even our acknowledgment of our sexuality underground. Such repression has shaped our sexuality into a secretive and hidden force, and we may find that it embarrassingly erupts at times least expected.

Because of wounds or shame we all seem to carry, we tend to misdirect our fears and misgivings onto the scapegoated persons who are survivors or offenders. Thus we seek to escape a sense of personal responsibility. We need to acknowledge that it is not only sexual offenders who struggle with an unhealthy sexuality. When it comes to recognizing sexual fantasies, for example, the difference is often less than we would like to think.

Rebecca: It takes guts for those who have not offended to say that they can have sexual fantasies about children as well. There seems to be this line between the ones who have offended and the rest who have not. That's not true. Nobody wants to be honest about their sexual fantasies. It would take a lot of courage for people who are not sex offenders to sit down and talk about their fantasies as sex offenders must do. I still wonder, though, Why does one person act on their fantasies, and another does not?

Becoming Aware of Unhealed Wounds

Gary: I know from my own experience that I had to come to terms with the fact that I had wounds. I needed help to become aware of this. I came to counseling and to the offenders' group, not even knowing I was angry about some things, let alone the awareness that I was not dealing with the anger appropriately. I needed to be able to talk about the events in my life, simply as things that happened to me, and then have someone say to me, "How do you feel about this right now?" For a long time, it was difficult for me to answer those questions.

Eventually I began to recognize when I was angry or sad or fearful. Counseling then helped me to put the history of those feelings into the context of my life. But this is a long process and not always smooth. Even now, more than three years later, my ability to recognize and process these feelings is still impaired. I still need help to do it, and I still need help to relate my current problems and fears to the events and emotions of my childhood and adolescence.

Survivors often block memories. This strategy allows them to function seemingly free of the destructive undercurrent.

Rebecca: When I was in denial about my past abuse, I could function in the church with no problem. I was president of the youth group and all that stuff. But now I have expanded my awareness and started a process of healing. I'm afraid of the Bible because of the way it was used in my abuse.

Iris: There was a time when the only phrase I could relate to in the whole Bible was "God hates evil."

It is understandable that many people would rather not raise unresolved issues. Their avoidance of them is a way of coping. Some individuals choose to remain numb rather than unleash what feels like overwhelming, uncontrollable pain and anguish. These walking wounded may be survivors or persons who offend. I also believe that people without direct experience in sexual abuse can have intense feelings about their pasts.

To describe the hurts of sexual abuse, consider the analogy of a deep wound. John Smith has suffered a deep cut that gradually begins to heal. The bleeding stops, scar tissue covers the gash, and skin starts to form. Beneath the surface, though, may be an infection that causes gnawing pain and discomfort and turns the scar red.

John Smith adjusts his movements to avoid bumping or in any way increasing the discomfort. He may become more and more preoccupied with protecting the superficially healed wound, and thereby have less ability to focus on other life tasks. His whole world revolves around preventing further damage to the wound.

The prospect of reopening and cleansing the wound with disinfectant is painful. John Smith wants to avoid that, for good reason. When he opens and cleans the wound, he can overcome the debilitating preoccupation with the hurt and begin healing. Perhaps a scar will remain, and maybe John Smith has reduced abilities, but he has overcome the debilitating preoccupation with the hurt.

Chip: Often the anticipation of the pain is worse than the actual pain itself. Our own fears frequently prevent us from cleansing the wounds properly. It takes an enormous amount of energy to carry unresolved hurts. When we acknowledge our hurts and work on them, then we have more energy that otherwise is used to keep control of all the issues that needed attention and healing.

Understanding Unresolved Hurts

Gary: I haven't come to fully understand some of my past hurts. For example, in my counseling I've talked about several incidents in which my mother perpetrated massive invasions of privacy and breaches of trust—things for which anger would be appropriate.

In one case, I remember I was angry at the time, but it was combined with fear, and the fear was more overpowering. Now those incidents leave me cold. Yet it must be a very angry kind of cold. My anger against women, which fueled my offending, did not grow out of nothing.

As mentioned elsewhere, the transition from unresolved hurts to healing is far from fast. The journey can be difficult for those who are close to someone on a healing journey.

Rebecca: It's really hard to be around a survivor who is healing, especially if you have your own issues. It's not easy to look back at unresolved hurts. The friends who you thought were going to help you have the same issues and cannot be around you to give you support. It's not a given that there's going to be anybody there to help.

Acknowledging that there are unresolved hurts is only a beginning step. Individuals also must understand the dynamics that cause hurtful cycles to recur. Such an analysis helps people come to terms with the messy and confusing whirl of emotions intertwined with their memories.

Chip: When you go back a couple of generations and start mapping things out, you can start to see similar patterns passing from one generation to another, as for example with alcoholism. If you don't get ahold of the root of those dynamics by examining the abuse and facing it, then you will likely follow through in a similar manner.

Look at all the people who have said, "I'm never going to be like my parents." Inevitably, you are in some way. It may not be exactly the same, but it usually ends up being just as hurtful.

Steve: I now have a better understanding of where I came from. I think everyone looks back, but this is especially necessary for a person whose family has had difficulties and whose life has become messed up. It has been important for me to look back at issues that I did not think had any impact on me, but I've learned that they did.

This gives me a better understanding of who I am. I like myself a lot better because of it. Yes, some bad things happened in my family while I was growing up. We did not live in the best of circumstances, but that is a part of who I am, and it makes me unique. Knowing that, I can live with it.

To maintain focus on their healing, those who have offended must understand and continue coping with their pasts.

Gary: Resolving my stuff from the past is a big part of what my recovery is about; it is what I did not address before. So if I don't get at those issues, then I am always in danger of going back to the familiar patterns that contributed to the abusive behavior.

Coming to Terms with the Wounds We Carry

Our past is always with us. We may yearn to bury our past and, like a caterpillar, be transformed into a butterfly. However, there are always aspects of the woundedness that resurface and remind us of our limitations. We want so much to be miraculously and instantly cured. We cannot cast the unclean spirits out of our past. They still bind us to some extent, and we want deliverance (Mark 5:1-20). Yet we can learn how not to let those spirits unduly control us now.

Gary: It is important for me to come to terms with the wounds I carry. This may include some confrontation with my family. It may also mean that I need to accept shortcomings, not only in myself but also in others. One of the hardest things for me to accept is that I did things a certain way because I didn't really know any better. When I apply this to myself, I know I must also be willing to look at my parents or others who have wronged me, and grant them the same indulgence.

People are often overwhelmed by the wrongs they have done, and they have difficulty believing they deserve wholeness or happiness.

> *Jimmy:* I do hear those inner voices that tell me that I don't deserve to be happy. Another part of me says that I do deserve to be happy, so I have to struggle with the other voice.
>
> *Rob:* Are we talking about attacking that voice that says you're no good or you're stubborn, or are we talking about embracing it? Embracing it in the sense that we acknowledge that it is a legitimate feeling, and trying to change the undesirable aspects of it. It's not necessarily something to fight or to squelch. It's something to respond to by asking, "What can I use positively from this message?"

Conclusion

We often avoid making ourselves vulnerable to others because we fear rejection or disapproval. Because of fear, we also fail to examine our unresolved pasts. Whether sexual abuse has been a part of our past or not, we still tend to hide our real selves. I believe it is important that we all take risks to discard the masks we create in a vain attempt to hide our fears and avoid our pasts. We need to talk things out with caring people.

Why is this so important? Consider the following:

> *Iris:* Because I have been able to be vulnerable with intimate friends, they then felt okay sharing their own vulnerability with me. I've experienced that with several people, and it brought quite a bonding and closeness through being vulnerable. Isolation is the problem for most people, so the good news is about being real. You can start being close to people again. You don't have those walls around you anymore, and that's freeing. It's good news for both survivors and offenders.

That is good news for everyone else!

9

What About Forgiveness?

Bill came to see me because he wanted to talk about a "family matter." The gray-haired grandfather looked very contrite as he told me about his situation. He acknowledged that he had a long-standing fascination with pornography. He also admitted that he had done and said many inappropriate and wrong things to his children as they were growing up.

Now his children all had their own families, and they were questioning whether the grandchildren would be allowed to visit him, especially for sleep-overs. "I've acknowledged my wrongful actions," he said. "So why can't they find it in their hearts to forgive and go on?"

Often we assume that when those who have offended acknowledge their wrongful acts, then things can begin anew. In most cases, this is not so. Acknowledging the wrong is the beginning of the healing journey, not the end. The victims want to feel that the wrongdoer understands how much harm was caused by those actions. They need confidence that the wrongdoer has taken steps to avoid any recurrence.

Like Bill, others seeking forgiveness often feel they are being mistreated by unforgiving and vindictive persons who reject their acknowledgment of wrongdoing. Like many other things, it is just not that simple. When we talk about forgiveness, we need to consider many additional factors.

Introduction

In the Book Reference Group discussions, no word was discussed as fervently as *forgiveness*. Why was that? Why does that word cause such strong reactions, such different views?

I tend to see forgiveness as one way to frame a path that leads toward the larger goal of healing. This chapter is about healing but with a focus on respecting the process. It aggravates victim-survivors when we tell them, "You *should* forgive." Forgiveness is not easy and may take a long time.

> *Rebecca:* It would be most helpful if we could get rid of the word *forgiveness* and create a fresh, new term to capture what is meant.

That may be a difficult or a long-range goal. Yet her statement does point to the strong undercurrent I felt while writing this chapter.

We must view forgiveness as a product of earlier stages, which include the confession of a wrong, remorse, repentance, restitution, and reconciliation. These steps can lead to forgiveness. The model previously outlined in this book uses different terminology, yet has a similar intent. The one who has sexually offended needs to acknowledge the wrong, accept responsibility, and then change behavior.

Book Reference Group members represented various roles. There were both "forgivers" and "forgivees." It was a challenge not to confuse the terms and perspectives, which varied greatly depending on one's connection to the issue.

In the church's understanding of forgiveness, the focus often seems to be on the victim more than on the offender. Victims are pressured to justify their refusal to forgive. This is most unfair. The Bible has much more to say about repentance than it does about forgiveness. We would be wise to follow that example.

Three aspects of forgiveness will be developed, based on discussion in the Book Reference Group. The first aspect is the inner psychological dimension. Many individuals spend a much time and energy on the question of forgiveness internally as they try to bring resolution through inner dialogue.

Second, the relational or interactive part may involve actions directed outward, toward the person who harmed. The individual is actively attempting to deal with the issues.

Finally, people hear messages from outside themselves that shape their thoughts and actions. Others call on them to forgive.

These three dimensions may vary greatly from one individual to another. As people journey, they may consider these dimensions simultaneously or in sequence. For some individuals, the journey includes forgiveness.

Psychological Aspects of Forgiveness

Much of our consideration of forgiveness is done within our mind and soul. It is an internal process that helps us work through pain to some form of resolution, sometimes almost entirely within our own thought process. For those who offend, the primary issue seems to be forgiving oneself. This was the first issue on the minds of the Book Reference Group as we began our discussion.

Jimmy: Are we talking about forgiving others or forgiving oneself?

Gary: That's where I always start. Somehow it always gets around to self-forgiveness. I can't seem to make progress until I do start to forgive myself for the things I've done. That's really hard.

Jimmy: The offender often feels that he doesn't deserve that forgiveness. But the way I look at it, if I go to counseling and work on myself and do everything possible to be different, then maybe I can forgive myself. If I don't, then I'm stuck in the past and don't progress, because I have this horrible thing on my shoulder. I feel I can forgive myself and go on, but it doesn't mean I ever forget what I did. Of course, when I go to talk at a church, I feel like I'm not as good as people around me, so maybe I haven't forgiven myself fully.

Surprisingly, self-forgiveness is also a long and difficult process for those victimized by sexual abuse. This seems unfair, but it is probably one more indication of the invasive nature of child sexual abuse. Responsibility, guilt, and blame are projected onto the very person who has sustained the injury.

> *Rebecca:* Being able to forgive myself is a big step in my healing and takes a long time.

Later we will consider how messages to "get on with it" create additional self-blame for victims about "not being able to do it right."

Survivors frequently are told that forgiveness is "for your own good." They interpret that as a message that they are falling short of what is expected.

> *Alexandra:* Early in my healing journey, I heard the theory that if you don't forgive, you drag it all with you, and it infuriated me. I feel relatively neutral about that phrase now, which is really nice. I do feel freer from my abuser, and maybe that's forgiveness.

Alexandra's internal process has worked toward some degree of resolution, but she still has some residue that can be difficult to face.

The group focused attention on those who had offended, wondering how they work on forgiveness in their own lives in ways that include the dilemma of those victimized.

> *Gary:* I'm thinking of my parents. There have been times when I was really angry about what they'd done. I kept going back to those events and getting more and more angry.
>
> Eventually I've come around to saying, "They were buried in their own things, and they did what they could, and I can't keep going back there because I can't change that now." So I try to sort it out and concentrate on what's ahead of me today.

That is a difficult process. The more intrusive and ingrained the wrong, the greater the challenge within to sort through the issues.

In the Book Reference Group discussion, there was a wide range of viewpoints and perspectives on forgiveness. It was evident that most of the women who were survivors found this a particularly unpleasant topic. They had devoted considerable "psychic energy" to it, often with no clear resolution.

The men who had offended also had a sense of uncertainty about forgiveness. They only agreed that (1) people should not pressure the victim, and that (2) every effort should be made to alleviate the guilt the victim may feel. Everyone agreed on one more thing—forgiving others is a very difficult process.

> *Iris:* I've been through many rounds of forgiving [my abuser], in other words, letting it go, leaving it. But the forgiving did not heal all my pain. Sometimes feelings would come up again. If I forgave last month and then feelings come up again, I say, "Okay, let's look at the wound again; I need more healing. Maybe I need to feel the rage again." When healing comes again and I feel restored, I feel the love of people and the compassion of God; then I can let it go again. So the forgiving is very much a process for me.

For Alexandra, forgiveness was complicated by others telling her about the difficult and trying childhood circumstances of her abuser.

> *Alexandra:* When I heard about what a rough life he'd had, I used to get really furious. It felt as if people were trying to cancel out my pain.

It is common for families and communities to try to minimize the harm by pointing to the traumas of the wrongdoer. That puts survivors, who need to raise their own concerns, in a difficult position. We definitely should recognize the traumatic experiences the offender has had, but we must separate them from his offending behavior. We must never imply to survivors that the offender's earlier life excuses the abuse he inflicted on others. Otherwise, the offender's traumatic experience and his offending behavior constantly cancel each other out. That impedes healing for both survivors and those who offend.

Rebecca warned about the limits of trying to determine where survivors are on their healing journey by assessing whether they have reached and mastered the forgiveness stage.

> *Rebecca:* The big issue for me is not forgiveness because I've been doing that all my life, and yes, I was doing it wrong because I thought it meant "forgive and forget." What I need is to place responsibility for the abuse with the offender. That is a major block for me because I have always taken responsibility, even when I was three years old.

Much of what has been said and written about forgiveness describes stages of forgiveness and outlines the steps of resolution. While such a model may provide a helpful framework, we need to listen to how people actually handle the issue in their own private worlds, which may vary greatly. It would be more productive for everyone concerned if we would spend more time demonstrating how much we care for those harmed by abuse. We need to spend less time trying to determine just how far along each one is on a hypothetical forgiveness scale.

How do you face the question of forgiving someone who has died? In such a case, the inward journey has a further complication: relational possibilities are limited.

> *Iris:* If I was expected to forgive and be reconciled with my grandfather, I'd be up a creek, because he died before I even recognized my feelings about his abuse. So I can't hear any words of regret and recognition from him about how he hurt me. In this situation, forgiveness can only be an inward journey.

At the same time, a victim may have opportunities to talk with other family members, write a letter or a journal, or visit a grave. She may process issues with one who offended against someone else but is willing to meet this victim (as in chapter 13, case 2).

We will come up short if we place much emphasis on a victim interacting with the one who has offended, or an offender processing issues directly with a victim. Healing and forgiveness might come through an interactive process, as the next section indicates, but this is not always the case.

Interpersonal-Relational Aspects

Consider the image of the wrongdoer who respectfully requests forgiveness, which the victim then politely grants. A handshake seals the matter, and life goes on. From what we have discussed so far, you can likely see that such a superficial resolution probably won't happen in a real sexual abuse scenario. It also represents a poor model for coping with any serious wrong. Something done that effortlessly becomes almost meaningless. It belittles the person wronged and gives the false impression to the aggressor that the wrong can be quickly remedied.

As we begin the discussion of interaction between the parties, I must offer some qualifiers. Some individuals find that such interaction provides a satisfactory avenue toward healing. I am not suggesting that interaction should be an expectation or obligation in all cases. That kind of external pressure leads to further victimization of those harmed by sexual abuse. (We will discuss that pressure more fully in the next section.)

Both victims and offenders are on a healing journey (which some may call forgiveness), and their paths may intersect. But it would be a disservice to suggest that they "must" work things out between them. That may be a relevant issue for consideration, depending on a number of factors, including how interconnected their future lives may be. Nevertheless, it is important for both individuals to choose their own direction.

In this discussion, we assume that the one who has offended has fully acknowledged the wrongdoing and is aware of the impact of those actions.

Alexandra: If you asked me point-blank, "Have you forgiven your abuser?" I would say "no," because he hasn't asked me for forgiveness or expressed regret. What I would want to hear from him is this: "Well, I've done a lot of thinking about this. Now I know why it happened, I understand what my motivation was, and this is what I am going to do so it doesn't happen again."

A member of a church community commented on forgiveness for a church leader who had sexually offended:

> Forgiveness is tricky. When Kenneth first confessed, I believe most of us were immediately ready to forgive him. The awkward part now is that while none of us had difficulty forgiving him for the sexual sins, he has not asked for forgiveness for the power plays and manipulation. Everyone was crying except him. I don't think I saw him shed a tear. That doesn't mean I don't appreciate the incredible loss to him and his family. But we didn't sense remorse from him, nor did we feel that he had a deep concern for us as a church. What we got was constant fighting from him at every turn and in every possible way. The man is very skilled.[1]

This example illustrates the complex nature of forgiveness and the importance of avoiding premature forgiveness, which can act as a religious window dressing to cover a much deeper and more widespread problem.

Frequently forgiveness is seen as a bartered exchange between the two parties.

> We buy too much into the notion that forgiveness is some sort of cash exchange between victim and offender. I may choose to interact further with my brother who abused me, but I'm more inclined to feel pity and compassion for the human condition than to experience forgiveness.[2]

A process of forgiveness can demonstrate a changing power dynamic, *or* it can further solidify the power and control that the abuser has had over the abused. Survivors often are concerned that when forgiveness is granted, the wrongdoer will stop taking responsibility for his actions.

Alexandra: It feels as if forgiveness is just for *them*. If they want it, then they need to ask and show they've earned it.

In this discussion of the relational aspects of power, we assume that the two parties are relatively equal in their relationship. Jimmy gave a personal example that underscores the importance of ensuring that the issues of power be dealt with appropriately:

Jimmy: I have never asked my stepdaughter, who was my victim, to forgive me. I told her how sorry I was that I hurt her, and that I shouldn't have taken her childhood away from her. At the time I felt that it was too soon for me to ask her for her forgiveness, and I didn't want to put her in that position. She's fourteen years old now and still too young for me to raise that issue with her.

Suppose we have a situation where two persons are not relatively equal in power and participating voluntarily. Then any forgiveness exercise can make existing or previous abusive relationships worse.

The social structure of the first-century Mediterranean world had a system where grades or classes of authority were ranked one above the other. In his article on forgiveness, Frederick Keene points out that in the New Testament, those with more power are instructed to forgive when another repents.[3] The gospel directs those with more power to forgive those with less power in the social structure. The Bible does not discuss the reverse situation, such as an abused child forgiving an abusive father.

A powerful example of this kind of situation occurred when Jesus was dying on the cross. From his position of powerlessness, he called on God (a higher power) to forgive his offenders. This illustrates that a person who has no power is not expected to (Keene would say *cannot*) forgive. While we may disagree with Keene's conclusions, I raise it here to point out that forgiveness is not a blanket commandment in the Bible, even though the religious community often assumes that it is.

Oppressive "Shoulds"

We now consider external factors that influence our understanding of forgiveness. Here my experiences most color my thoughts. I have so often seen the effects of the prescriptive "shoulds" that I find it difficult to weigh the merits and demerits equitably. We need external support for our internal belief systems. We want such support to significantly strengthen our emotional security. However, when we hear messages from others that do not promote our health and instead contradict our inner feelings, we experience a major conflict. I often see that conflict when considering forgiveness in the context of sexual abuse.

The Bible is a source of tremendous encouragement and hope for many people. Tragically, because of misuse, the Bible has become a barrier to healing for many. This is nowhere more evident than with the term *forgiveness*. We must avoid using the Bible to command victims to forgive offenders. We can offer the Bible as a rich resource for healing rather than as a club to beat the wounded.

Book Reference Group members varied on whether what others said supported their healing or hindered it. Iris spoke of the positive role the church had played in assisting her.

> *Iris:* As a Christian, I knew that somewhere down the road, forgiveness was something I would want to do. I had compassionate people around me who didn't force the issue. They were willing to wait until I was ready.

Rebecca was less positive about the church's role. Church people did not help her because they quickly focused on forgiveness:

> *Rebecca:* Why bother having a specific point of forgiveness? Why not just have a healing journey?

> *Iris:* Forgiveness for me is not a one-time experience. In relation to my grandfather, I've gone round and round on the issue. The reality is that I needed to open the lid on my

sexual abuse issues after I had forgiven. Instead of closing down the lid by saying, "This agenda is dealt with; I've already forgiven," I said, "Yes, I have forgiven, but I need to look at this agenda again, by going to a deeper layer."

I have come to forgive again and again as often as my healing journey required. Maybe seventy times seven! Each decision to forgive enabled more healing to happen.

Rebecca: How is that different from healing?

Iris: I don't think it is. Forgiveness is part of the process of healing.

This exchange was like much of the discussion. People come from varying points and have differing responses to formulas that tell us what to do. That does not need to be a problem if everyone respects differing viewpoints, as did the members of the Book Reference Group.

Iris: I was nervous coming here tonight because I knew that I wanted to say some things about how forgiveness has been a liberating thing for me. But I was afraid that I would come across as being manipulative on the subject of forgiveness, come across as suggesting that people should look at something that they're not ready to do. I have no desire to do that. But I can't be silent about forgiveness being a liberating thing for me, so I want people to know about the liberating perspective.

Other group members nodded their understanding.

Conclusion

My understanding of forgiveness is shaped by the notion of a grain of sand in an oyster. Over time, the friction of the sand creates a pearl. As a victim of sexual abuse, forgiveness means coming to terms with the struggle that has ensued for me, and then doing something differently to alleviate the negative outcomes and to create a pearl.[4]

This quotation suggests that creative outcomes can occur, even though the initial event was devastating. I do not wish to further obligate or place expectations on anyone to forgive. I want to focus on supporting and challenging wrongdoers to become accountable for their wrongs. This focus may set the stage for a healing journey that includes forgiveness.

In working with sexual abuse, I rarely initiate a discussion of forgiveness. I prefer talking about future relationships if they are desired. Perhaps we look back later to see what has transpired regarding forgiveness.

In summary, I believe forgiveness is best understood, not as a process with specific steps, but rather to look back on later and say, "Yes, healing happened." Some people may label that healing "forgiveness."

10

A Caring Church Responding to Those Who Have Offended

Now when Job's three friends heard of all these troubles that had come upon him, each of them set out from his home—Eliphaz the Temanite, Bildad the Shuhite, and Zophar the Naamathite. They met together to go and console and comfort him. When they saw him from a distance, they did not recognize him, and they raised their voices and wept aloud; they tore their robes and threw dust in the air upon their heads. They sat with him on the ground seven days and seven nights, and no one spoke a word to him, for they saw that his suffering was very great. (Job 2:11-13)

This account of Job's friends offers a moving example of a caring response to someone in dire distress. They arranged to come together to support him in his time of need: he had lost his children and possessions. (His wife survived.) Sensing his torment and deep anguish, they sat with him in his grief for seven days without saying a word.

We often focus on Job's friends' subsequent response— their attempts to blame Job. At first they were supportive; then they undermined that role with their arguments, ones with which we can identify. Job's friends believed that Job was responsible for his misfortunes. They exhorted him to confess his wrong so the matter could be rectified.

Job's friends give us positive examples of how to respond in times of trouble and examples of pitfalls to avoid. Their first response shows genuine commitment to Job. They went to be with him, they sensed his deep hurt, and they sat with him for seven days in silence. What an amazing ability to empathize with him in his grief! Often being with someone is more important than talking or doing.

In our fast-paced society, things go much more quickly. When there has been harm or tragedy, we move swiftly to determine the "truth" and make quick responses. Job's friends demonstrated patience, empathy, and quiet support during the first seven days of their visit. We can better develop those responses in our churches and in broader community circles.

Avoiding Judgment, Acknowledging Denial

Like Job's friends, we want to decide who is to blame for the misfortunes of others. This is probably more evident in sexual abuse matters than in any other area. Consider how victims are judged. Whatever the characteristics of the victim or the perpetrator, the surrounding community often minimizes the responsibility of the offender by implying that the victim was irresponsible or careless.

Why do people blame the victim? Iris offers one answer:

> *Iris:* It is so difficult for most people to identify with someone who is vulnerable. That means that they have to face their own vulnerability. Few people want to think something this bad could happen to them.

If we can blame others for their own ill fortune, we can avoid facing the reality that sometimes bad things happen to good people. Job's story is a troubling and instructive example of that reality. According to social scientists, the tendency to blame the victim comes from a deeply held belief that people use to push away their personal fears. "If I can find a way that the victim contributed to her or his own tragedy," the reasoning goes, "then I can cling to a false belief that if I just avoid that action, that tragedy will not hit me."

Both survivors and those who have offended find it hard to gain acceptance and be heard. However, it is often more difficult for the victim-survivor to receive a hearing than an offender, whether the offender is totally denying the accusation or seemingly accepting responsibility. Why is that the case? One member of the Book Reference Group explained:

> *Iris:* It is very important to state clearly that the issue is power. People automatically side more with a person who has abused power than with the one who has been abused by power. It doesn't make a difference whether it is a church leader or not.
>
> I have experienced this. When I openly shared, I thought, "Surely people will side with me and believe in what I am disclosing." I was so surprised that people had a hard time initially drawing near to me. At first they don't offer wholehearted support to the person who is so vulnerable. They have to learn to do it. Thankfully, many people do.

In many ways, our churches and communities are still in denial about abuse, and there is pressure on those involved to participate in the denial. If the offender denies the accusation, then there is a great burden on the victim to "prove" her or his claims. Because we do not want to acknowledge the abuse, we would rather believe that the accusation is not true.

> *Steve:* Looking back at the time when I was first accused, I was in a whole lot of denial. I blamed my daughter. "She did this to me." I had a whole list of reasons as to why things happened.

The pressure to say "It's not so" comes from family members and affects both victims and offenders.

> *Steve:* A lot of family members wanted to pretend it didn't happen or to gloss it over as really minor. My dad is awful that way. I think he still hasn't accepted what I've done. He

throws glib Bible answers at me, and I reply, "If that's in the Bible, you'd better show me where you find it."

A survivor gave her perspective:

Rebecca: There seems to be more support for the offender if he is denying that anything wrong happened. People in my family would have a harder time with somebody who admitted to sexual abuse than somebody who did not. If my brother said, "Yes, I did it" [sexually abused my younger sister], then there would have been much drawing aside of frocks, so to speak.

Gary: I think I understand that, because if somebody says, "Yes, I did it," then there is an aura around you. You could be still wanting to abuse, or you could do it again. But as long as you are denying, then that's not a problem because the abuse is not real.

In addition to our denial, we have a strong tendency to want to patch things up quickly. All those involved in sexual abuse report having experienced inappropriate pressures or being offered simplistic or judgmental answers.

Alexandra: One issue I have with church people is the way they use biblical Scriptures to give easy solutions. As a survivor, it's not helpful for me to have someone give me a lecture, saying, "This is what you should be doing." What I needed, and still need, is for church people to support me, to help me find my own way, and to sit and talk with me instead of coming across as the "expert," or [speaking] from an "I know best" position, or hammering me with "this is what the Bible says you are supposed to do in this situation."

One of the biggest things I struggle with is to gain a sense of personal power; that's been difficult for me all my life. It does not help me to develop a sense of personal power to have that stuff handed to me. I'm curious to know if that parallels the offender's experience.

Steve: Yes, it does, at least partly. Shortly after my offending came to light, and when my ex-wife and I were first separated, the pastor gave my ex-wife a book entitled *Forgive and Forget*, and the church people put a lot of pressure on her to do that. At the time I actually thought it was wonderful. But now I realize that it wasn't right.

Judgmental comments and attitudes are destructive for both victim and offender. We must refrain from easy answers. It is more helpful to come with openness, willing to learn from those in pain rather than attempting to impose pat solutions.

A church community may feel torn between opposing views on a sexual abuse issue. The church needs first to provide safety for the victim, and *then* to cope with the wrongdoer's needs. For example, church leaders can ask the wrongdoer not to attend Sunday morning services. Church leaders can offer alternate · arrangements to meet the spiritual needs of the offending person. It will likely be difficult for a church to take such action and ask the offending person not to attend. However, we must not sacrifice the security of the victim to accommodate the offender. We can see this as a logical consequence, usually temporary, resulting from the wrongful acts he committed.

It is difficult for persons not fully informed about abuse to understand why safety for the victim is so important. Often there does not appear to be any "danger" to the victim from the perpetrator, particularly in cases where the abuse ended long ago. In family settings, there often has been an ongoing relationship between the abused and the abuser without apparent discomfort.

That is, however, a superficial view of the situation and does not fully take into account the impact of childhood trauma. Children develop ways to cope, to gloss over their pain. However, when the hurt is reopened, even if they are adults, much of the original terror returns and must be faced. If survivors are to feel supported and safe in church communities, they need church leaders who respond sensitively to their struggle.

Steve: I think the offender should be pulled out of the direct church setting, and the survivor should be asked what she or he needs. The survivor needs to be supported in the church; she should not be pulled out of church because she did not do anything wrong.

Iris: That's how I see it, too. The offender can still be cared for. He is like somebody going to the hospital: the patient in the hospital doesn't drop out of the church, and the church members go to the hospital and care for that person. But the victim, I feel, should have the freedom to be in church.

With this level of support, the church body is sending a clear message to the person offending and to the survivor about the significance of abuse issues. Such support tells the victims that their needs are being addressed, and it indicates to those who have offended that sexual abuse is being dealt with more seriously than it was in the past.

Openness or Privacy in Processing Abuse?

By now the reader is aware of my conviction that we must deal more openly with sexual abuse if we hope to reduce its frequency and its impact on our church communities. We often use the term *confidentiality* to highlight the need to respect the privacy of vulnerable persons who have shared personal information. However, we need to recognize the limits of confidentiality, particularly regarding child sexual abuse. We must not place more children at risk to maintain confidentiality.

Sometimes there is a fine line between "confidentiality" and "secrecy." The typical scenario in churches involves a situation where the sexual abuse is already well-known in the congregation. Sometimes it is kept "confidential" to avoid harming the reputation of the church in the broader community.

Rebecca: I came from an evangelical background, and I learned there that you don't let on outside the church that anything is wrong inside the church. Otherwise, "people are not going to want to be saved." So if something bad happens, you sit on it, and keep the lid on it. [They say,] "We can't let the sinners know that these things are happening in the church."

Iris: I think the church would sooner err on being too secretive. The issue is secrecy; that's what keeps abuse alive, so I want to fight secrecy. I agree that not everything can or should be processed in public. But I believe it's important to state the facts and to be discretionary about the details of the abuse. We can't hide the reality that this person who has offended has a failure.

Sometimes religious beliefs reinforce the ban on discussing sexual abuse matters within the church.

Rebecca: In the church that I was a part of, there was a sense that God spoke through other people. So if someone gave a message saying the matter is closed and dealt with by God, then that was viewed as God's voice. If you bring it up again, then it must be the devil that brought it forward. In other churches, now, I've seen a lot more realism, a lot more people being held accountable, and awareness that healing takes place over a period of time. That's why I'm quite hopeful.

Some things are changing as churches have learned more about sexual abuse and how to handle it more effectively.

Iris: Years ago I told my small group that I had been sexually abused. I showed them the paper I had written that I wanted to use to disclose [the abuse] to the church, and they said, "We can't allow you to use the words 'sexually abused.'" It would have been acceptable to say "perceived sexual abuse." I had to go to a counselor to get some power behind my words.

In those days, I found myself saying, "The church is a little dumb, and I wish they were smarter." I'm getting ready to say to my present church, "If we want to grow, we will need to be aware of sexual abuse issues because people are going to come with these issues. If we want churches to grow, we are going to be facing sexual abuse. I think we should be ready."

The people involved in the disclosure of sexual abuse will vary, depending on the situation. Usually, all people (including children) who could be affected should be informed about the sexual abuse. Thus, for example, if an uncle molested his niece, everyone in the extended family should be told. The purpose is to ensure that all victims have been identified and to allow everyone to take whatever precautions they feel necessary for their own safety and the safety of their children.

If the abuser was a pastor, everyone in that pastor's congregation would be affected and should be told about the abuse. Also, the official group that issues ministerial credentials must be involved and know (see chapter 6).

Support and Accountability

We must combine support and accountability in responding to those who have offended sexually. This is a significant aspect of the church's role. I will outline what these terms mean and explore the church's role as part of a broader pattern. The church does not direct the process. The church participates in the process with many agencies and individuals who have ongoing involvement with the person who has offended.

When persons who have sexually offended begin to face their offenses, the treatment typically involves both group sessions and individual time with a qualified therapist. The group provides a place to learn from the experiences of others who have struggled with similar issues. The individual can apply learnings to her or his own life. The *peer review process* (see description in appendix 2) is one way to focus the problem areas and to identify possible solutions and positive directions.

In *individual therapy*, the person has an additional setting where the experiences picked up in the group can be reviewed in greater detail. That increases the learning possibilities. Counseling also provides a place where new and different kinds of responses can be developed and learned. Then the individual can take those new responses back to the group. The group operates as a practicing laboratory, a safe place to take risks.

A third setting, a *support-accountability group,*[1] provides a safe and comfortable place for the individual to share what he has learned in treatment with a wider group of significant persons. Such a process further undermines the secrecy that is at the heart of the destructiveness of sexual abuse.

The support-accountability group serves two purposes. First, this group provides a setting where someone in a treatment program can explain what he has learned. He can share those learnings with people who are aware of the past and can give support based on insight and understanding. People in treatment gain a new awareness of the issues, and they recognize the value of putting their learning into words to solidify it.

Second, this group also educates the participants about how best to avoid more sexual abuse in their families or communities. Participants hear about the issues and the situations in which offenses took place from someone who has offended. Thus they gain a greater understanding of the reality of sexual abuse, how vulnerable children are, and how best to work at prevention.

A support-accountability group could include all or some of the following people:
- from family: spouse, ex-spouse, sibling, aunt, uncle
- friend(s)
- victim advocate representative
- child protection worker
- pastor
- from criminal justice: police officer, probation officer
- individual therapist
- someone from therapy group
- employer
- neighbor or community representative
- individual support volunteer

As this sample list shows, there is a wide range of possible members who may have differing agendas. Yet they have a common concern to ensure that there is no recurrence of the abuse. The group destroys the secrecy that has enshrouded the abuse. It requires someone who has offended to discuss the offenses and learnings openly, within the bounds of confidentiality. This open sharing is quite a different way of being for the individual and is essential for healing. I think it is a reasonable request to make of persons who have offended and are part of church communities or families.

The key participant must be willing to be involved in such a process. Why would someone voluntarily agree to such a level of scrutiny? One reason might be to demonstrate concretely the desire to make changes. He may also want to avoid isolation and loneliness.

Often the circumstances surrounding disclosure of the abuse have led to an increased sense of isolation on the individual's part (loss of family, and loss of other social supports). The support-accountability group provides a tangible way for him to be connected to other people at a deeper level. Individuals who participate in such groups typically find that, in the process of being held accountable, they are given a significant amount of support and affirmation for their willingness to be open.

The support-accountability group is most useful after the person has, through individual and group therapy, taken responsibility for what he or she did. If there have been years of minimization and denial, the offending individual will need much reinforcement to make appropriate self-disclosure. This newly learned ability enables him to participate in a support-accountability group.

Usually a support-accountability group meets several times a year. In consultation with a church or agency staff person, the group leader invites other group members, to ensure that there is a balance of perspectives represented. In the initial stages, the participants need a clear explanation of the process by someone who understands the various dynamics and can set the appropriate framework. Participants must engage in and commit themselves to the process. In the long term, their involvement is a significant factor in enabling the person who offended to solidify the learning and to avoid returning to nonproductive and potentially abusive patterns.

Being represented on such an accountability group is one way for the church to become involved on more than a superficial level. Steve described the positive role of his church in his accountability process.

Steve: I didn't experience a sense of community until after my offending became public. Then I discovered how many friends I did have. They responded in unique ways. There were people who regularly wrote to me when I was in jail. Others would call or visit. Before I was sentenced, several individuals asked, "How's it going?" People would say, "What's going on with your family? What's happening in court? How are your children doing?" That was really neat. I had never before experienced that kind of concern and connectedness in the church.

When I was released from the correctional institution, I moved to a new community and lived with a Christian couple who had connections with my home church. They included me in their Bible study group. I did not tell the group why I was in jail until after the third meeting; they accepted it well and never came back on me about it in a negative way.

As the Book Reference Group discussed this issue, Alexandra wanted to know more about it.

Alexandra: Were those questions to you different from the usual questions that are a part of social gabbing? I'm curious, because it sounds as if you felt the freedom to talk honestly, and maybe you sensed that they wanted you to share information?

Steve: I think that's true, because a lot of them didn't know much about sexual abuse. In fact, I arranged for Mark to come and talk to the Bible study group. That opened things up further for them to ask more questions of me. There were two couples that I was closest to and could talk to on a fairly open basis. If I was feeling really lousy, I could tell them.

Alexandra: If you had not been to the treatment center at the correctional institute and you came out to a new church where people didn't know about your past, wouldn't that have been quite different? I'm asking because my experience of church has not always been that positive. Often it seemed to me as if people were being superficial and going through these little exercises that they did because they were in church.

Steve: No one came up to me directly and said, "Are you having difficulty sexually?" But their concern was evident. I did talk openly with several close friends and a counselor, and then later I was involved in a group. It was important that I had those people there, because otherwise I would have lacked that accountability.

This discussion has promoted support and accountability for the person who has offended. It is equally important to support sexual abuse survivors. To promote restorative healing, we must provide parallel healing supports for survivors and offenders.

Advocacy

In abuse matters, those directly involved need advocates. This is true for those who have offended and for survivors. It is difficult for persons who have offended to deal with their issues, particularly at the beginning, without an advocate to assist in raising or responding to the many issues.

If the church does not choose an advocate, someone may assume this role without accountability to the church. Sometimes the advocate will be a pastor. However, in most situations, it is better to have a person with a lower profile in the congregation, particularly if the victim is also part of the congregation. This arrangement will free the pastor to provide care to others.

Advocacy for those who have offended is different from advocacy for survivors. I am talking about advocacy for those who take responsibility for their offenses, not for the wrongfully accused or those in denial. Advocates do not excuse or minimize the offenses. They assist offending individuals in dealing with the real issues they face when they begin to deal with the enormous harm caused. Frequently such offenders have suicidal thoughts and fears.

Most of us find it difficult to talk openly about deep emotional matters, particularly if they involve something as shameful as sexual abuse. Because people in such situations frequently do not feel comfortable speaking, they need someone they trust who can speak for them.

Being an advocate can be difficult. Often others in the church community don't want to hear the information on someone else's behalf. The advocate must maintain a supportive and nonjudgmental attitude toward the person who offended. At the same time, the advocate must be honest and forthright about any personal concerns that arise.

In a general way, the church can act as an advocate for all those affected by sexual abuse by demonstrating awareness of sexual abuse. Through the teaching program of the church or specific mention of sexual abuse in worship, liturgy, or prayers, the congregation can give courage and hope to those who struggle with sexual abuse issues.

Nurturing Faith

At the heart of the gospel message is a call to follow the path of Jesus. One of the main tasks of the church is to foster growth and understanding of what it means for every believer to live a Christian life. Such nurturing in faith is also for those who have been abused and for those who are abusive. It certainly can be a valuable resource of connection and solace through the stormy journey of recovering from sexual abuse.

Providing for Corporate Healing

When sexual abuse comes to the surface in a church, the ripples or waves are far-reaching. The abuse raises issues for individuals about personal experiences long buried. Sexual abuse has an impact on the whole congregational body.

Iris: The church needs time and space to grieve and process its group issues. If someone in a church discloses, that opens a group wound. The wound is not just for those individuals.

Chapter 7 outlined a framework for offender healing. This included the acknowledgment of the offense, taking responsibility, and changing subsequent behavior. Can those principles help bring healing to the whole community of faith? I think so.

If our church community can acknowledge the reality of sexual abuse, we offer immense comfort to those who carry the burden of abuse. By declaring our clear expectations to those who have offended, we also offer hope and restoration.

If the community is to accept responsibility, we must over time deepen our understanding of the widespread garbage left behind after sexual abuse. We must break the community silence that discourages its disclosure and consider the following questions: What ideas about sexual abuse have we absorbed from the broader society, without evaluation by the church? Have important values like family solidarity and lifelong marriages contributed to the unwillingness to deal with issues directly? Are women as well as men empowered in our congregational life?

As we tackle such questions, we must maintain our fundamental values and beliefs in a way that allows us to address abuse openly, justly, and restoratively.

Changing our behavior has corporate implications as well. We also need to consider other questions: What have we changed as a church body that shows we have learned from past mistakes? Are procedures and policies in place to prevent abuse? Is there a process to deal openly and honestly with future abuse issues? By answering such questions, we create a safe and healthy congregational climate.[2]

Concluding Comments

The church's role in responding to those who have offended was a challenging topic for the Book Reference Group. Their closing comments included the following:

Steve: It was a really good discussion. But in telling my story in the detail that I did, I now feel a lot of pain in facing the realities of what I have done. Last Sunday I had one of those days I haven't had for a long time. I wanted to be alone, yet

I didn't want to be alone. I'm feeling somewhat like that tonight, too, talking about this stuff.

I think it's about accountability. It's a question that keeps haunting me. To whom am I really accountable? Who is asking me if everything is okay? So I may be in denial about some of that stuff. There's a lot going on, but I still think it's a good process.

Chip (co-facilitator): I feel sad and I feel angry. I think a lot of people are afraid and misinformed and generally want to handle situations. But out of pure ignorance, they respond badly. It worries me when others are the recipients of [harmful responses]. That experience can push them away from the church and from being connected to God, which can be a key to healing.

Gary: I was just thinking about Mount Cashel [Orphanage in St. John's, Newfoundland, Canada, where Christian Brothers sexually abused young male residents during at least two decades]. The church and government decided to accept responsibility for the sexual abuse of residents by numerous priests. I think that is really good. But I feel cynical. Maybe both of those institutions acted as they did because they were afraid they would get bad press. I really wish we could find churches that deal with sexual abuse without hurting people again.

Jimmy: I guess I'm responding to what Steve shared tonight about accountability. Who am I accountable to? Before, I was accountable to my wife and daughter, but that's all finished now. So where am I going? I'm not involved in a church. I guess now I am only accountable to the members of my treatment group and to myself.

Alexandra: I feel a bit discouraged, and that's familiar. At the same time, it's quite positive for me to talk to people, because all of you are in touch with this issue. My discouragement comes because I want answers. I want to hear, "Okay, here is the best way to do it. Let's talk to the church and get them to do it."

As I sit and talk in this group and listen to other people, I realize it is really complex. There is no easy answer, and that is where I get discouraged. I appreciate the sensitivity and the attention I heard people paying to the survivor when they were talking, especially in the context of the church. I have to say, though, that the bottom line for me is that I don't want sexual abuse to happen. I don't like to deal with it, and I am tired of dealing with it. I just don't want any more sexual abuse.

Rebecca: Today as I went to give a talk about sexual abuse, I was thinking, "This last week has been sheer hell. So who am I to go off and talk to somebody?" I've heard from all of you over and over again that what is most helpful is telling my story. So I need to concentrate on the positive things that have been happening.

Iris: I'd like to add to my earlier comments that were rather negative about the church's response. My husband and I found four people, two couples, who have supported us for about a year. One couple was fairly knowledgeable about abuse issues and secondary victim issues; the other couple was not as aware, but they were eager learners. They kept saying, "We are honored that you would trust us with this information and share it with us. We want to learn." That was very positive, and those were leaders in the church, along with their spouses. I will never forget it.

Guidelines for Handling Sexual Abuse Issues in the Church

In a church setting, various situations arise which require a response from church leadership and other participants. It is vital that leaders first consider seriously how to respond and to resist ignoring or avoiding the matter, as was done earlier. In this section, I am assuming that the sexual offending does not involve persons in leadership positions (on that situation, see chapter 6).

After following any mandatory reporting requirements, the church's role in most cases will be to handle spiritual concerns and interpersonal relationships in the church. Other persons, such as therapists or court officials, will be involved to deal with other aspects of the healing process. It is essential that the people who are providing leadership be experienced in handling sexual abuse issues. While church leaders may prefer Christian counselors, if the counselor does not have experience with or awareness of the dynamics of sexual abuse, it may be important to consult with other counseling resources.

1. Considering Legal Action

A. *Reporting requirements*. As mentioned, it is a legal requirement in most jurisdictions in North America for professionals who have knowledge of suspected child abuse to report it to the appropriate child protection agency. Even when the child who was abused is now an adult, the perpetrator's access to other children may be cause for concern. It is preferable to contact the child protection agency for information about when reporting may be required rather than making a personal determination of what is appropriate.

B. *Criminal or civil action*. Usually there is no requirement to report sexual abuse to the authorities if the person victimized is now an adult, even though the offense(s) occurred when she/he was a child. (It is not necessary to report on that victim's behalf.) It is important to provide the victim with a range of options for pursuing justice. The victim needs information about how to proceed with possible criminal sanctions. Similarly, the victim may pursue a civil lawsuit, although there may be time limitations for beginning such an action.

Often the use of criminal or civil court action may not seem to be a viable option within a family or church. I introduce it here to emphasize the increasing use of the courts in such matters. I also feel that possible legal actions often motivate persons who have offended to take responsibility for the harm they have done.

2. Providing Safety

Concerns for safety are relevant not only if the person who offended continues to be involved in the community and/or church. If such concerns are present in the community, it will heighten the need to deal with safety concerns. Here are some questions to ask for determining whether there are safety concerns:

A. Are the victim's needs for *physical and psychological safety* being met adequately over the necessary course of time during which the abuse is being processed?

B. Is *spiritual and pastoral support* available for the victim? Is the support free of unhelpful expectations for quick reconciliation and forgiveness?

C. Is there *respect* for victims who may wish to delay processing issues for a time?

D. Is there *regular consultation* with those who are providing support and accountability to the wrongdoer, to ensure that there is ongoing progress in confronting the underlying issues and patterns?

E. If treatment is prematurely ended by a person who offended, have sanctions and consequences been put in place to handle the *safety concerns of survivor(s)?*

3. Making the Process Open and Broad Enough

It is awkward, uncomfortable, and painful to deal with sexual abuse. As a result, many people prefer narrowly focused and covert responses. The following questions help develop a framework that is more open and comprehensive:

A. Has the person who offended dedicated adequate *time and commitment* to the healing process? A person who violates and offends another person, has developed that degree of disregard and disrespect over a period of years, perhaps decades. It is unrealistic to assume that he will quickly change his attitude and behavior. Typical treatment programs involve weekly individual and group participation for a period of eighteen months to three years. The commitment to change is a lifelong process.

Recently I spoke with Bill, a Christian who has taken seriously his need to seek spiritual as well as psychological healing. He says that he began his healing journey five years ago and is now no longer in an active treatment program. Yet he still confronts temptations within himself almost every day that could lead to re-offending. Bill has developed a prayer ritual and relies on a spiritual mentor to provide him with the ongoing support he needs.

B. Has there been due respect for the *confidentiality* of the wrongdoer while defining limits to that confidentiality and avoiding inappropriately privatizing of the issue?

C. Is there an extended emphasis on the *spiritual issues* central to the loss of respect for self and others? For example, how does one find hope when the awareness dawns of the devastating impact of sexual abuse on the victim?

D. Is there *coordination* between the role of the church and the roles of other agencies or individuals who are part of the accountability and healing process?

11

Facilitated Dialogue

If I had tried to set up a family meeting with a psychologist or someone like that, I would have had all kinds of resistance from my family. A family conference with a dialogue facilitator was less threatening.

Looking back, I saw it [the conference] as a springboard for my family. We agreed, "Let's put the cards on the table and get on with it." For members of my family to travel up to five hundred miles to talk about past sexual abuse in our family, that was amazing. And all nine family members attended.[1]

Survivors can choose a variety of ways to be open with those who have harmed them. One method is working through a criminal or civil trial in a courtroom. Some survivors use a direct approach through letters or a face-to-face meeting. Often this is done with much forethought and support from the community, spouse, friends, pastor, counselor, and others. This chapter outlines another method that some survivors choose—facilitated dialogue. We will consider its advantages and possible pitfalls.

Why Facilitated Dialogue?

Structured dialogue provides a setting in which two persons in a conflict, persons with relatively equal power and control, seek to resolve a past hurt with the assistance of a neutral third party (one or more persons). Such dialogue can offer a worthwhile alternative to a civil or criminal court proceeding, which may be unsuitable for a variety of reasons. As discussed in chapter 4, in the courts the control rests with the presiding judge and/or jury.

Facilitated dialogue, on the other hand, gives the participants more control. The participants set the stage for discussion, and they develop ground rules. Either party can step back, slow down, or stop the proceedings. That is not possible in the court system, particularly the criminal courts.

I have explained the principle of personal empowerment throughout this book. Dialogue empowers both the victim and the person who offended. For people devastated by the aftermath of sexual abuse, protected dialogue can be a significant way to regain a sense of control. For those who have offended and understand the impact of their actions on their victim(s), facilitated dialogue provides a way for them to take responsibility in practical and concrete ways. That response can demonstrate their new awareness.

I participated as a facilitator in about twenty-five cases over the past five years. Typically, I dealt with abuse that occurred many years earlier—sometimes thirty or forty years ago. Usually the victim contacted me. Most often she or he wanted facilitated dialogue to ensure that other family members would be protected from abuse by the same person. Often victims stated that they came forward then because the one who offended had children (or grandchildren) approaching the age the victim was at the time of the abuse.

Facilitated dialogue helps wrongdoers and their victims address the abuse. I present it as an option, to provide variety and choice in coping with sexual abuse. Such an option must not become a "should" for either victim or offender.

Later in the chapter, I will identify significant cautions and describe situations where such dialogue is not appropriate. The facilitator must be someone who understands the principles of facilitating such dialogue and the dynamics of families. This helper must have a solid awareness of sexual abuse. A facilitator enters into the intimate hurts of families only when there is suitable preparation and true openness for the task.

A Model for Open Dialogue on Sexual Abuse

Since 1990, our agency has received a variety of requests for mediated or facilitated services. We responded by developing a particular model. We now look at the goals for this model and the various phases in a typical case.[2]

Goals

• To provide a supportive environment in which individuals affected by sexual abuse can address the harm caused by this behavior.

• To provide an alternative to the criminal justice system's adversarial approach to cases of sexual abuse.

• To promote healing from the traumatic effects of sexual abuse.

• To counteract the secrecy and shame surrounding sexual abuse by providing a safe environment that encourages openness, honesty, and accountability.

• To provide an empowering experience in which all individuals affected are given an opportunity to be heard, to have choices, to have an impact on the process, and to negotiate any requested compensation.

• To build community by engaging supportive circles for various parties healing from sexual abuse.

• To promote individual responsibility for behavior that has harmed others.

• To facilitate reconciliation if desired by those involved.

• To provide a link to other treatment approaches.

Initial Inquiries

Most of our initial inquiries come from people who call to ask about mediation service. They ask general questions about how it might apply to a particular situation. Usually the victim calls. Sometimes she or he has had no conversation about the abuse with the person who offended. That person is most often someone in the extended family or in the community.

We ask the caller several questions: (1) Whom do you want with you for support? (2) How can we contact the person(s) who offended? (3) What are your goals for such a meeting? We suggest that the callers gauge their readiness for such an undertaking. We inquire about what steps have been or are being taken on the healing journey.

We ask the caller to visualize two scenarios: First, imagine the person who offended giving either a positive or a negative response to the request for a meeting. Second, imagine your reaction.

Since the facilitated dialogue cannot go ahead without the cooperation of both parties, we must prepare the caller to cope with either scenario. Sometimes there is six months or more between the initial inquiry and follow-through by the caller. This interval demonstrates that an attempt to pursue dialogue is not a spur-of-the-moment decision but part of a longer-term plan and movement toward healing.

Separate Discussions with the Parties

The next stage is a meeting between the facilitator(s) and the male or female victim. The victim offers a full account of what has transpired and discusses his or her goals in pursuing the matter.

There must be three-way agreement before proceeding to the next stage. The initiating party, the person who offended, and the facilitator(s) must agree to go on. The facilitator must feel confident in a positive outcome for all parties. This is based on factors hard to measure. The facilitator must assess the sincerity of the parties, particularly the ability of the perpetrator to take responsibility for the act(s). The facilitator must determine the ability of the parties to shift the focus of the meeting from a determination of what happened to problem-solving about next steps.

The facilitator's role is to guide the process. In the face-to-face meetings, the facilitator supports all persons. Hence, each victim-survivor and offending person should bring his or her own support person(s).

The facilitator offers the victim various options for contacting the party who offended. Sometimes, if the abuser is a sibling, the victim can write an open letter to the family, suggesting a date and time for a meeting;[3] she can also invite all family members to contact one of the facilitators to talk further about the process. The invitation is intended to allay any fears or misgivings various members have about the process. In other situations, the facilitators send a letter to the person who offended, explaining the request and inviting him or her to contact a facilitator to discuss the matter.

Normally I recommend that the facilitator talk to the various parties involved. That gives each participant a personal sense of the facilitator and his or her role; it builds advance trust between that professional and everyone involved. If the participants have confidence in the facilitator, there will probably be a positive outcome. Sometimes family members live at a great distance. That makes it difficult to have prior personal contact. In such cases, the facilitator can build trust through telephone conversations.

The facilitator meets with the person who offended. It is important that the individual who offended feel safe and supported so he or she can participate in opening up this sensitive topic. That person offers his account of the abuse. The facilitator listens carefully to see if there is substantial agreement on events. If the account differs from the victim's version, those items are noted. The parties may negotiate further about what will be discussed face-to-face. That meeting can go on if there is not full agreement on every aspect, but those differences need to be openly identified for all parties.

The facilitator works with the person who offended to refine the agenda for the face-to-face session. The agenda was developed in the meeting with the victim. The facilitator reviews it with the offender to assure that it is mutually acceptable. The facilitator also assesses what motivates that person to be involved in the meeting. The facilitator invites the individual to arrange for his or her support person(s) to attend.

At both meetings, a waiver is introduced and explained. The waiver says that the party who signs it acknowledges that he or she is voluntarily participating, that a solution cannot be imposed on either person; and that the facilitator or records kept by the facilitator will not be involved in subsequent court proceedings.

The purpose of the waiver is to avoid a situation where someone could use the dialogue to get an admission of guilt, which they then might use for another purpose in a different context. Facilitated dialogue is different from the criminal or civil justice systems; each has a different way to handle admission of guilt. Finally, the parties must understand that participation in dialogue does not mean they can't go to court in the future.

When the participants and the facilitators agree, they are ready for the next step.

Face-to-Face Meeting

I prefer to have structured dialogue sessions involving additional people besides the principal parties. There are a number of reasons for this.

First, with more people involved, there is less tendency to polarize the issues. Often others who know both parties and have their confidence and respect can play a bridging role. There is also less pressure on either party to respond to every issue in the framework for the session.

Second, structured dialogue heightens the long-term impact of the abuse. Frequently in extended families, various members are aware of the sexual abuse at various levels. It is quite different, however, to sit in a room and hear the actual statements by the victim. Even though the abuser may try to belittle the abuse, the presence of others who are supportive and nonjudgmental will help to reinforce for the abuser the impact of his or her actions. Similarly, those people supporting the victim can hear the abuser taking responsibility for what he did.

Everyone in the room hears what agreements are made.

Because of their ongoing involvement, they will act as ongoing moral "enforcers," to ensure continuing accountability.

The atmosphere at the beginning of the session is sometimes cool and tense. There may be awkwardness as people gather. The people may know each other well, but they might be estranged and divided into two camps. Sometimes, though, I have been surprised by the seemingly congenial and friendly atmosphere.

The physical surroundings are important. The sessions are held at a neutral location that does not favor either party. I prefer an informal living-room atmosphere. We usually serve coffee and allow time for informal chitchat as people arrive and settle in. Specific concerns from a member or members about safety or proximity with others at the meeting are identified in advance and then arranged with the knowledge of everyone. We try to avoid unexpected events that can be unsettling.

The facilitators have a significant role in setting the tone. One or both have already met with or spoken to most of the participants. Their modeling can underscore the seriousness of the undertaking without setting too stiff and formal a tone. I encourage having both a female and a male facilitator. Both facilitators initiate items for discussion in a balanced way. Thus they model that both men working with persons who have offended and women working with survivors can cooperate with families to address issues of concern.

The meeting follows the prepared agenda. Typically, the person who initiated the meeting begins with a prepared statement that outlines her or his goals for the meeting, along with a statement of the harm experienced. Then individuals can ask questions of clarification or make general comments about what has been shared. People are encouraged to express feelings rather than philosophical or intellectual statements.

Frequently the person(s) who offended responds with a prepared statement. Then there is another opportunity for questions and responses, again guarding against the tendency to rationalize and intellectualize. Sometimes the facilitators need to remind participants that certain comments or issues are best saved for later in the meeting, depending on the circumstances.

Often family members tell the victim they are sad about the abuse she has endured. They also frequently voice surprise when they hear the details and declare that the impact of hearing it directly from the victim is powerful. They affirm the person who offended for his or her willingness to face the issue.

After the principal parties have shared and others have responded, the group moves through items on the agenda. Additional items may have been added at the beginning of the meeting. On key points, we often go around the circle and invite everyone to comment or to pass. This discourages anyone from dominating the session and encourages the expression of a variety of opinions necessary for balance and bridging. Individuals often state that they had felt torn and immobilized by the conflict, but feel relief and hope because the matter is being acknowledged and processed.

During the discussion, individuals may express concerns about commitment to future action. For example, someone who has offended sexually may agree to further counseling. A plan is made to confirm that counseling is taking place without violating confidentiality. Sometimes families need to discuss an upcoming family event, such as a wedding. Their decision may not be written in a formal agreement. However, it is important that everyone understand what the agreement is. The people in that group must guarantee that the planned course will be followed.

There may be items that cannot be resolved. It is not critical that every issue be completely settled in the meeting. However, there must be a mechanism to pick up issues in the future. We try to empower the group to work toward the support and healing of all parties and toward the resolution of harm.

I am still surprised by the freeing effect that people experience when they can talk openly in a protected setting about something as secretive as sexual abuse. If the person who offended acknowledges responsibility, then this structured form of dialogue enables those directly involved to develop solutions tailored to their unique circumstances.

Following Up the Session

In most cases the facilitators follow up by telephoning the various parties involved, to consider with them what has been addressed and what feels unfinished. Sometimes either party may deal with issues further in counseling. Some use other ways of handling dynamics in the extended family.

The goal of the face-to-face session is to open up greater dialogue in the family and to help the extended family be a resource for the victim or the offender. The group decides ahead of time what they will do if the facilitated agreement is broken. Typically, the group discusses this at the meeting. Everyone knows the plan that will be put into action.

A man who was abused by an older brother shared the following post-session comment:

> It was quite effective that there were ten other people in the room [brothers, sisters, parents], and all of them were affected by the discussion. People were now free to say to [the older brother], "We don't feel comfortable when you sleep at our house, or when you offer to take the kids out for an ice cream." The meeting allowed people to share concerns that had been under the surface for a long time, and that was positive.[4]

When Facilitated Dialogue Is Not Appropriate

In sexual abuse situations, the facilitated dialogue model outlined above could be used inappropriately, with potentially harmful results for all concerned. I will clearly state six situations when structured and protected dialogue *cannot* deal with sexual abuse situations effectively.

1. Do Not Use It to Determine Validity of Allegations.

If both parties do not acknowledge the abuse, the process can become stuck in arguments that further victimize. It is possible to work in a situation where there is not full agreement on the issues. However, it is essential that the wrongdoer have a basic willingness to bear responsibility for the harm done. Otherwise, particularly if close family members are included, the wrongdoer can try to convince a "jury of peers" that the actions were minor. He may insist that the allegations of sexual abuse stem from mutually agreed-upon sexual activity. This dialogue method would be similarly inappropriate in addressing totally unjust accusations.

2. Do Not Require Involved Parties to Participate.

Families can put subtle or direct pressure on the victim (and/or wrongdoer) to "get reconciled" for the good of the family. Such pressure does not empower the victim or the offender. The persons facilitating the process must be aware of how families exert undue pressure. The facilitators should go on with the process only when they believe it is the victim's choice. In addition, the facilitators must sense authenticity and sincerity in the person who has offended, particularly about accepting responsibility.

In a church or Christian family setting, the pressure to forgive and reconcile can be counterproductive. Such arguments do not promote lasting healing, as discussed in previous chapters.

3. Do Not Use It to Keep the Abuse a Secret.

Criminal court proceedings have some potential advantages; one is that they open up the issue of sexual abuse. There is a public record that specific charges have been made by the police. Those charges will result in a guilty plea or a trial that will determine whether the charged person is guilty or not guilty. A dialogue process is by nature less public. However, it is essential that the "affected public" (families with children who could be at risk) know about the sexual abuse. All parties, including the facilitators, must be satisfied that relevant persons are aware of and/or included in the process.

4. Do Not Use It If Any Parties Doubt That the Offending Person Will Carry Out an Agreement.

Unless the parties who participate believe that what is agreed to will be carried out, the process likely will not work.

> *Rebecca:* I don't know what you do in your dialogues. But if my brother who abused me sat across from me, he could say all the right words, and I wouldn't believe him until there was a track record of responsibility being taken.

If people in the group do not trust the abuser or other family members or both, there is little likelihood of a positive outcome.

5. Do Not Use It with a Significant Power Difference.

People exert differing degrees of power over the people around them. This dynamic depends on a variety of factors. For example, a twelve-year-old daughter living with a father who sexually abused her would not have enough independence to speak her mind freely.

However, if the confrontation and/or subsequent dialogue took place twenty years later, when the daughter was thirty-two and quite independent of her father emotionally and financially, it is possible that the power dynamics would have shifted. In such a case, facilitated dialogue might be an appropriate choice. She could decide how she would feel comfortable in interacting with him. She could decide how much or little contact he would have with her children.

Similarly, when there is a difference in power because of the respective roles of the parties, facilitated dialogue is not appropriate. An example would be a minister who sexually abused a member of the congregation. There is a significant power imbalance in that relationship. Governing bodies to whom ministers are accountable frequently use mediation to avoid validating the complaint.

In this example, the minister breached responsibility to his or her employer and to the church member who was abused.[5] After the investigation and discipline have been handled, there may be an opportunity for facilitated dialogue between congregants and the *former* leader of their church.

6. Do Not Use It as a Family Therapy Session.

The session should be *therapeutic* for participants, but it is not family therapy. Family patterns and dynamics are complex and evolve over many years and generations. The facilitated dialogue may stimulate family members to address issues that they become aware of during the session. However, family therapy is a longer process; its goals involve restructuring patterns of interaction in the extended family. Structured dialogue has a more practical, short-term, and specific agenda.

Conclusion

This chapter has presented a model for using facilitated dialogue in dealing with sexual abuse. Most of my experiences involve situations where the victim and the offender are part of the same family or extended family and yet somewhat separate. At the time of the meeting, they are sufficiently independent of each other and relatively balanced in their power to address the issue productively.

Sometimes people suggest that in sexual abuse matters, facilitated dialogue should replace the criminal and civil courts entirely. Such a practice could evolve, but first we must operate with the knowledge and experience we have. In processing an issue restoratively, we want to avoid situations that cause further harm to the victim or to the offender.

12

Restorative Justice in Difficult Cases

Streets of Fear: Siege mentality and suspicious stares on street where residents fear a recently released pedophile now lives.

Frightened ex-con in hiding, pastor says.

Findings on child-molester study a shock.

Workers protest molester's return.

Fear relatives, not strangers, pedophile says.

Headlines such as these have shaped our perceptions of sexual abuse and feed a mood of despair and hopelessness. Such sensational language colors our perceptions of sexual offending. The majority of sexual abuse cases are not the pictures painted in the media. Nevertheless, in many instances the accused person molests again, and the trauma increases for victims and their families. This especially is true since sex offenders and their victims usually know each other or are from the same family.

I remember the guilt and failure I felt when I was a probation officer and someone under my supervision offended again. Recently, as survivors of sexual abuse have told me about their pain, I have again felt guilty and discouraged.

The reader may wonder how the principles and approaches of restorative justice can be applied to difficult cases. Frequently people say, "That's all well and good, but what would you do about this case?" What typically follows is a scenario that seems to defy resolution.

This question is interesting for several reasons. First, existing, traditional approaches cannot resolve the stubborn cases, so we expect that other, newer models will not solve all our problems either.

Second, the question avoids an analysis of the factors that lead to abuse. Many people who have offended have experienced years of abuse and neglect before they harmed individuals and destroyed the community. It is naive to expect that a new approach will readily fix the problems of such entrenched abuse.

Finally, the question reflects the hopelessness that society feels about dealing with sexual abuse. In this chapter, we will consider situations that I find difficult. One way I cope with obstinate cases is by holding onto a hope that we will focus more on early intervention. I hope we will openly address sexual abuse so we can reduce or even eliminate the occurrence of stubborn cases.

There are three scenarios that are hard to manage in a satisfactory way, three kinds of difficult cases. In the first situation, the accused completely *denies* committing sexually abusive acts. In the second, the accused partly acknowledges and partly denies. I call this the *"yes, but"* defense, and it occurs frequently. In the third, the responses of the person accused *cannot be trusted*, based on experience, because of repeated offending. Let's consider these in greater detail.

Denial

Gary: Any case where there is denial is difficult. Someone who denies responsibility or denies there is a problem produces two negative deeds: first, the refusal to validate the victim's experience; and second, the refusal to start on a path of correction and recovery.

Why would someone do this? My experience is that the process of recovery is slow and painful, and I think in some ways my counselors would tell me I don't know the half yet. I believe that someone who willfully denies what has been done does so because the pain of self-examination is still much greater than the anger or fear that sustains the denial.

The man in my office was personable and articulate. He was interested in the work of the agency, asked how it was funded, and shared things he had experienced in his work. He was thorough and detailed in providing family background information. When we began to talk about the charge that had led him to my office, he was similarly definitive and precise. He provided considerable detail and concluded by saying that the "so-called incident" simply had not happened. He could only imagine why the babysitter would have spun this complete fabrication.

He was quite convincing. With difficulty, I have learned to be skeptical of initial impressions. Without information from the alleged victim, it would be easy to assume that this was a rare case where the accusation was a complete fabrication.

I dislike being a detective trying to find the truth. It is not my nature or training to distrust what others say. It is more significant that after years of working with those who offend, I cannot discern which ones who deny the offense will ultimately acknowledge their acts and which will, rightly or wrongly, maintain their innocence.

Faced with this dilemma, I approach the situation by being as honest and forthright as possible. I acknowledge that I did not witness the alleged offense; I do not have magical tests or formulas to determine truthfulness. I also state that the alleged offense might not have happened, but that my years of experience in dealing with such matters suggest that it probably did occur.

The stakes in such a situation are significant. It is unjust when wrongful acts are not confronted and acknowledged. It is devastating for a victim to be abused and then to be abused again when the first abuse is denied. Even worse, such denial continues the festering of our corporate wounds, as families and church communities. At the same time, our notions of fairness and justice prohibit us from wrongfully judging someone who might be innocent.

There are alternatives to my approach. Many counselors challenge the "untruthful" statements. In some cases, the counselor may "wear down" the accused by this method. My belief and experience are that it can also create added defensiveness and determined denial. Therefore, I tend to avoid the harsh and confrontational approach.

What about the opposite approach of accepting the denial without raising questions? This tends to ensure that we do *not* deal with sexual abuse! We are unaware that our silence or lack of comments will have an impact on a person accused of abuse. Individuals who strongly want to avoid facing an issue may interpret the lack of a comment as silent support for what they are saying.

The reader may prefer a more "objective" way of dealing with this situation, carefully weighing his word against hers, to establish beyond reasonable doubt what occurred. Reasonable doubt is always present. But it is unfair to possible victims to ignore that the abuse probably occurred, as recognized in the vast majority of cases. We have turned a blind eye to abuse for so long, and we are still facing the consequences of our corporate denial.

It is often useful to think first of the victim. What is the impact on the victim when she or he names the abuse and has it dealt with openly? The initial revelation of the abuse is usually quite painful and overwhelming for the victim. Why would anyone go through such an ordeal except to get relief from a deeply held truth?

Listeners may be tempted to provide unqualified support for a person who has been accused. That decision is often based on incomplete and one-sided information. Such support without confrontation can be most unhelpful. Whether offered by a counselor, pastor, family member, or friend, such support generally makes it more difficult for the person who has offended to acknowledge the truth.

Another form of denial can be an "inability" to remember the alleged events. There may never be an outright denial, but the individual will consistently state that she or he has no recollection of the event. We need to let the issue unfold, to give the accused time to think about and respond to the allegations. This is often difficult for those who love and care for the accused. However, this approach may not be advisable if the safety of a child is involved.

Sometimes when there has been excessive alcohol or drug use, the individual's response may be close to the "yes, but" approach. There is sometimes a link between addiction to alcohol or drugs and sexual offending. In other instances, the individual has an addictive personality trait that may be expressed through a sexual addiction.[1]

Allegations can be false or inaccurate. However, in the vast majority of cases that I have handled in more than a decade, the accusations have been true and accurate. It is understandable that persons close to the accused will have difficulty. It is excruciating to feel split loyalty, trying to decide whom to believe. When I am in that situation, I find it helpful to think of the many women, children, and men who suffered because issues were not faced in the past.

Yes, But

The majority of persons accused probably will acknowledge that the event happened but will provide some explanation that minimizes their actions. Some typical responses follow:

1. "It Was Just Touching."

A widely used minimization is that if there was not complete sexual intercourse, then the abuse was so minor that it was almost insignificant. Victims of such acts see it quite differently. In chapter 2 we discussed the impact of abuse on the survivors, including the destructiveness of "just touching." Here we focus on the perspective of those who offend.

I have learned that men who have offended usually have convinced themselves that it was "harmless." Their judgment is distorted by their focus on immediate self-gratification and by a corresponding lack of concern about how the act will affect the victim.

2. "She Approached Me."

People who offend often create images of themselves as passive victims who made valiant efforts to "fight off" the seductive and sexually explicit advances of aggressive children, and ultimately lost the battle. That is not the way it happens. Clearly, these individuals are misinterpreting the child's intentions. Children are by nature affectionate and trusting; adults must not abuse that trust.

Children are also curious and look to adults to teach them how to manage their developing sexuality. They need messages from adults that their bodies and their sexuality are precious gifts, that they have choices about touch, and that they need guidance about how to express their sexuality. If a child does make inappropriate sexual advances, it is up to the adult to stop the activity, affirm the positive boundary between adult and child, and teach the child healthy expressions of sexuality.

For example, a nine-year-old daughter may be sitting on her father's lap and watching television. She may turn to him and try to kiss him on the mouth, as warmly and fully as the adult actors on television. It is the father's responsibility to draw a boundary. He may pull back from such a kiss and say, "Only Mom kisses me on my mouth that way." He may also offer an alternate way for her to express her affection toward him, like a kiss on the cheek.

When someone says, "I was approached," I sometimes respond, "Suppose a child comes to you, sits on your lap, reaches into your pocket, takes out your money, and then goes to the store and spends it. Would you say, 'I was approached by the child who took my money: what could I do?' " Not likely!

Probably the adult would stop the child and point out the need to respect other people's property. Why should the response be any different when there is an inappropriate sexual advance? We need to face our confusion and taboos about sexual expression and teachings and make changes to stop future sexual abuse.

Finally, when both parties are adults but one is in a position of power or authority, the same approach is essential. Suppose a woman has been counseled by her pastor concerning sexual difficulties in her marriage and then becomes involved in a sexual relationship with that pastor. She will probably feel a great guilt and self-blame. She may wish to sort out her feelings and issues in a safe setting.

We must recognize the power imbalance. That pastor used intimate information about a vulnerable person for his own sexual gratification. Therefore, the pastor must be held fully responsible. The focus must be on the fact that the pastor is responsible for crossing appropriate boundaries. Side issues, such as the state of the victim's marriage (or the abuser's marriage) should not detract from this central issue.

3. "Everybody Knows She's Sexually Promiscuous and Dishonest."

It is not unusual for those who sexually offend to be moralistic and judgmental about the alleged sexual promiscuity of their victims. They may try to capitalize on a young woman's reputation for being easy, or the common idea that a divorcée or widow is desperate for sex. They commonly excuse themselves by saying the victims were "asking for it" by the way they dressed. This form of denial and victim-blaming can lead to some odd logic.

A man described himself as quite religious. He said he had sexually abused his daughter and sons because it was contrary to his beliefs to commit adultery by engaging in sexual activity with someone outside his family. Better to commit incest than adultery!

A person who molests a young male may berate his victim

for homosexual tendencies, implying that the responsibility is with the youth rather than with the mature adult. In many situations, the child or adolescent who was sexually abused begins to act out sexually and is then blamed for being promiscuous. This is most unfair.

We do well to remember Jesus' compassionate responses to "sexual" sinners (cf. John 8:11). Furthermore, the victim's sexual acting out is a striking reminder of how persons who have greater life experience, knowledge, and power can shape a situation to the detriment of others who are vulnerable.

4. "It Wouldn't Have Happened If My Wife Would Have Had Sex with Me."

This statement again shifts responsibility to someone else and avoids looking inward for the real reasons for the abuse. It also reinforces the myth that a male has the moral right to have his sexual needs met by some other person. Few individuals, male or female, are free from the effects of this destructive stereotype.

This argument is inappropriate. Sexual abuse frequently takes place while the person who offends has an ongoing sexual relationship with another partner. Sexual abuse does not occur simply for sexual gratification. It involves power, manipulation, jealousy, revenge, and a whole host of emotional needs. The abuser expects the victim to take care of his emotional needs.

Repeat Offending

Gary: For some reason, I've been dreading this discussion of re-offending. I don't know why. Maybe it scares me because some part of me says there is no ultimate solution to sexual abuse and sexual offending. It will always be with us. Maybe it scares me because I feel in my heart how close I came to being an "extreme" case. Even now I feel the shadow side of me that is angry, that is hateful and has an impulse for violence.

I don't expect this will ever go away entirely, so I have to learn ways of accepting this as a real part of me and coping with it. I'm still learning what this means, learning that my attempts to circumvent this shadow side do not always work, and learning that suppressing it does not work at all. But the part of me that chose life and recovery doesn't like this shadow part of me and has a hard time facing it.

It's painful to recognize this sinister side. It makes me feel less human, even though intellectually I can say this is part of being a human being. It is even more painful to accept and integrate this aspect of myself. It is helpful to know that I can integrate that angry self rather than splitting it off and allowing it to offend, and that integrating it will diffuse some of its energy. But the process still hurts. The angry, resentful part of me still indulges in self-righteous resentment, and the selfish part of me still demands attention.

Dangerous offenders? Repeat offenders? I have a feeling that some of them are so numb, so afraid of feeling their true emotions, that they cannot break out of their pattern. I have to have compassion for people like that, knowing how hard it is for me to break through to my underlying emotions. My head says "Okay, let's do it," and my heart shrinks in fear.

A dangerous offender, a person in denial, lives through hell every day. To unconditionally love someone like that must take enormous courage. I don't think I could do it, and I'm an offender who understands some part of that hell. Certainly society hasn't shown an ability to do it.

There is growing concern in North America that sexual abusers are dangerous. The Canadian federal government and numerous states in the United States have developed legislation in response to public concern about repeat sexual offenders who assault children. Let us set aside the question of whether this legislative effort is really tackling the fundamental issue of widespread sexual abuse. It does indicate a desire by legislators to label and to appear to be responding to the problem.

Because such laws are focused on strangers who repeatedly offend, they do not touch the majority of cases—persons who sexually offend within the context of trusting relationships.

Many volunteers in prison ministries understand the needs

and issues of incarcerated people. It has been important and necessary to sensitize the church to persons in prisons. Now the church is taking its first steps to becoming sensitized to the issues and concerns of the victims of sexual crimes.

Prisons are a much more visible mountain of human misery and pain, and that focuses our response more directly. The victims of crime, sexual or otherwise, are in their own isolated, individual "prisons" throughout the community. Hence, we have more difficulty seeing their needs for compassion and sensitivity.

Involvement with inmates presents a challenge because of the possibility of ongoing relationships after a prisoner's release. Well-meaning Christians have sometimes relied on simplistic answers that have failed to address sexual abuse effectively. They have sometimes unknowingly placed others in the church community at risk. I believe we can find the solution, not by isolating the persons who have offended, but by appropriately sharing information to decrease the possibility of future harm.

I dislike the negative and punitive system on which prisons are based. I want to work toward an approach to crime and conflict that makes prisons unnecessary. However, there are persons whose actions are so hurtful that the court decides it is not safe to let them move freely in the community. We cannot ignore the risks they present to past victims and potential victims. Prisons that separate persons from their community connections are a stopgap measure necessary at this time, while we develop other more effective options.[2]

Applying Restorative Justice Principles

I want to review the restorative justice approach to crime, particularly for sexual offenses. I will comment on its relevance and limitations. I am aware of the visionary nature of these restorative justice principles.[3]

My goal is to foster a dialogue that creates better ways to deal with past offenses, and that builds healthier communities and churches where sexual abuse is prevented. We must keep working toward that goal.

Respect

We should treat participants in a way that values their worth as human beings and respects their right to justice and dignity. My ability to respect is challenged when persons do not take responsibility for their actions. It is easy for me to become impatient and disrespectful because they are not open.

I maintain my commitment to the restorative justice principle by reminding myself that disrespect on my part is shortsighted. It does not encourage the accused to move toward the goal of acknowledging the offense. When those who are accused are treated with respect, they are more likely to acknowledge the offenses. With such an acknowledgment, there will be a more satisfactory resolution for everyone.

Obviously, we must be as concerned about showing respect to those who are harmed as to those who harm.

Integration

It is a restorative justice goal to integrate the person who offended into the community positively. However, it is unwise to integrate certain individuals at the expense of others. For example, it would be difficult to reintegrate someone who offended another church member if that meant the victim would be hurt and perhaps unable to attend church. It is essential that community integration be done in consultation with all affected groups.

In some cases, there was no community support system or a previous integration attempt failed. Therefore, more restriction may be required. We need to develop better understandings of what conditions make integration work for the community, for the one who offended, and for the survivor of the abuse. We need better understandings of where and at what level restrictions are needed. If an offender is not connected to a caring community, there is a high risk that he or she will re-offend.

Democracy

This principle rejects labeling, condemning, and authoritarian controls. Democracy is a process that encourages participation and empowers people to develop their own goals and internal controls. It is easy to become impatient and try to hurry the process along. However, that often takes ownership away from those most directly affected.

Our impatience can hinder persons who sexually abused from developing responsibility. We must find ways to hold them responsible without taking over their journey toward accountability and healing. We must allow survivors and those who have offended to guide us in responding to their needs and issues.

Advocacy

This principle affirms the importance of fair process. Because of our revulsion at sexual abuse, particularly in difficult cases, we may struggle to make sure we protect the rights of those who offend. When people deny their actions, we may be tempted to react with harshness and denial of rights. That may be effective in the short term, but it will not achieve the long-term goal of respect for fair process.

A harsh approach compounds the confusion and damage surrounding sexual abuse. It delays our communal healing. Particularly in the difficult cases, I find that by maintaining advocacy for the rights of the accused, I ensure that I maintain my own standards of fairness. That enables me to continue my work.

Honesty

This principle calls us to treat participants in an honest and open manner. We inform them of procedures and processes that can lead to the restoration of broken communities.

In accord with this principle, counselors need to tell participants what procedures are likely to occur and advise them of their options. A counselor also needs to be honest when having doubts about the accuracy of someone's report that an event did not happen. This can be shared in a friendly and open way that allows for further discussion. Participants must also be aware of limits on confidentiality when children, past victims, or possible future victims are at risk.

Group Feeling

When the Book Reference Group considered their discussion of this topic, they all reported how draining and depressing it had been to discuss something so painful and with so little resolution.

> *Iris:* I went home from that meeting feeling profoundly empty. We discussed questions that did not have definitive answers.

Guidelines for Coping with Difficult Cases

Increasingly, charges are laid and the courts have been dealing with persons who have committed sexual offenses against children. An increasing percentage of persons in prison are serving sentences for sexual offenses. Upon their release, they return to their home communities or to new neighborhoods where their past is not known.

Where those individuals have not taken responsibility for their offenses and the harm caused, there is an increased risk that they will re-offend. If they have destructive lifestyle patterns, including the use of alcohol or drugs, there is a further increased likelihood of repeat offenses.

Sometimes these individuals are drawn to religion and seek out cleansing for their past sins. It is important for pastors and other church leaders to hold in balance both the transforming power of God in the lives of all persons and the need for all of us to work out our individual faith with "fear and trembling."

In appendix 3, an intensive community based model called "Circles of Support" is outlined that appears to be an effective approach to difficult cases. In addition, certain questions are helpful in guiding approaches in difficult matters:

1. Considering Legal Questions

Such questions will vary depending on the situation. It is always important to face the question of children who may be at risk and the need to report the matter to child protection authorities where the risk exists.

If there is a known past pattern of offending, it is important to get information from parole or probation officers on the legal restrictions. The written consent of the person who offended is likely required to obtain that knowledge. If the individual is unwilling to grant consent, then those guiding the process have a logical basis for curtailing her or his activities that could place other persons at risk.

I have found that in such a situation it is often most effective to go to the parole or probation office with the person who offended, and ask the pertinent questions in his presence.

Many jurisdictions now make provisions for longer-term control of persons who have sexually offended. When we collaborate and cooperate with the officials responsible for such supervision, we can use these provisions creatively and effectively.

2. Providing Safety

Ensuring safety for those who are vulnerable must begin with the person who has offended. Pivotal is his willingness to accept and engage in appropriate accountability procedures. This establishes the necessary climate in which to begin. One method increasingly used in treatment programs for men who have offended is the development and monitoring of a relapse prevention plan. This approach is borrowed from relapse plans for persons addicted to drugs. It involves the offender noting the past behaviors that led up to previous offending. Then specific detailed activities are developed to halt the cycle at every point along the way.

Individuals from churches who are involved in circles of support or accountability groupings need to be aware of such procedures and support the professionals administering them.

In addition to *physical safety*, survivors need a *psychological* sense of *security*. There can be a range of options to consider that include asking the person who has offended not to attend certain events, or having someone designated to be with the person who has offended throughout a specific meeting. Group leaders can work out in advance where people will sit to avoid uncomfortable proximity to others affected.

In a similar way, with enough discussion and negotiation about other family gatherings, a satisfactory arrangement can be achieved to handle the safety concerns of all persons involved. Often, the difficult part is how to do this without making the person who has been victimized feel guilty or unreasonable for stating legitimate safety concerns.

3. Taking Account of the Needs of All Persons

As previously mentioned, the ripple effect reaches many persons who sometimes have little choice or ability to react to their predicament. Other agencies and individuals may be involved at least in the early stages of community release to provide some form of supervision. Their focus will be largely on the person who offended.

The church can play a significant role by advocating for more sensitivity to the perspectives of other persons affected in some way by the presence in the community of someone who may be at risk of re-offending.

4. Being Willing to Limit Involvement of a Person Who Has Offended

Increasingly the courts are providing mechanisms of long-term control for those convicted of sexual offenses. Persons from the church community can work cooperatively with supervisory agencies to reinforce the existence of external controls. The church can accept and support the controls and still continue to relate to the person who offended in whatever form. Thereby the church models compassion toward those who have offended and sensitivity to those who have been victimized either by this individual or by someone else.

I have argued that it is necessary to stay involved with people who offend, and to include them safely in the community rather than to isolate them. At the same time, it is essential that communities have clear and realistic expectations that must be met by persons who offended as part of reintegration into the broader community or church.

Church leaders can assist in setting those expectations and

in limiting the individual's involvement in accordance with those expectations. At the same time, leaders can welcome further discussion, in this way, they invite ex-offenders into relationship without undermining the need for accountability and changed behavior.

13

Restorative Justice Working

This chapter offers three situations where the principles of restorative justice were used effectively. They provide examples of the variety and range of possible applications.

Case 1 illustrates how people responded when a sexual offender was released from prison into their neighborhood.

Case 2 includes excerpts from an ongoing dialogue between a survivor and a person who had offended. This dialogue took place over a period of more than a year.

Case 3 describes a community prevention-education event planned jointly by survivors and those who have offended.

As said before, any particular example will not necessarily fit every individual, church, or community. They do give me hope and energy as I work in this challenging field. Read, question, and consider.

Case 1: A Neighborhood Meeting

My experience with Sue[1] and her neighbors illustrates how we as a community might respond to matters of sexual abuse. Sue called one late summer day. She had discovered that a person she labeled as a pedophile had just been released from prison and was living in her neighborhood. Sue had heard alarming and conflicting information from neighbors and wanted to know what they could do about it.

Sue had already had a lengthy discussion with the police. "Yes, they were trying to be helpful," she said, "but they were guarded in their comments, for reasons of confidentiality." She was very concerned for the safety of her children and the many other small children in the area.

Her information included Bob's name and the names, address, and telephone number of his parents, where Bob was living. He had been released after serving a six-year prison term. Sue knew Bob had been convicted eight times, and she assumed he had repeatedly re-offended.

Later I discovered that there were indeed eight convictions for sexual abuse. Those eight offenses had been processed in one court case as a series of misdeeds. He was convicted of all eight crimes. Yet there is considerable difference between eight separate court dates with repeated convictions and an accumulation of eight charges dealt with at one time. Records show that the offender is less likely to re-offend when eight offenses are handled at one time than when eight offenses are tried separately. Even so, in both scenarios eight persons are victims, and the reality of the trauma to those individuals does not change.

Sue said she was sure it would only be a matter of time before Bob would re-offend, based on what she had heard and read about pedophiles. "So what can I do?"

I suggested that it might be helpful for me to contact Bob. I offered to advise Bob that information about him was circulating and to ask for dialogue on neighborhood concerns.

Sue agreed, and we discussed the limits for my call. I would not reveal who had called me other than to say it was someone from his neighborhood. I would ask his cooperation in setting up a meeting with him, several support persons, and probably four neighbors, to discuss their concerns.

Bob was surprised that there was already widespread awareness of his presence, since he had only been released for five days. He understood that there might be concerns, and he quickly agreed to interaction with the neighbors. We discussed how this might take place, and we set a tentative date for an evening meeting a few days later.

After a series of calls between Sue and myself, and Bob and myself, we agreed to a number of points. The focus of the meeting would be constructive, not volatile. The neighbors would outline their concerns, and Bob would respond. Anyone involved could refuse to respond to a particular matter or could respond later. Caroline and I, agency staff people, would assist in the discussion, to give structure and safety. We would meet at the agency office, in an old house with a large waiting area that doubled as a meeting room. That offered neutrality and comfort.

Two police detectives would attend. While not directly speaking about Bob's case, they could provide valuable background information about the criminal justice system and court proceedings. I told them they would be present chiefly as an information resource. I also acknowledged that their presence could add to participants' feelings of security.

Generally, I recommend an advance face-to-face meeting between the facilitators and the others involved to build a greater sense of trust. However, in this case it did not happen.

Even with careful planning, there are surprises. On the day of the meeting, Sue called to say that *eight* people definitely wanted to attend. She explained that there had been much discussion in the neighborhood, and she felt that the people who wanted to come represented varying concerns and valuable areas of experience. "They have been well briefed regarding the need to speak in a rational, controlled manner," she assured me. "There will be no hotheads."

Bob was understandably nervous about the extra people, but he agreed. I suggested that Bob might want an additional person or two to accompany him. When I called Sue to advise her that Bob agreed to the change, I shared my impressions about Bob's positive and open stance that I had sensed throughout our many telephone conversations.

Caroline and I arranged the chairs in a circle. We had coffee and lemonade in the kitchen. We set the air conditioner on high to cool the room on that hot, muggy summer evening.

Bob arrived first, accompanied by his parents and Joan, a

support person from church. Soon the neighbors arrived as a group. As planned, they had met at Sue's home to prepare their presentation. When I shook hands with Sue, she said there were two additional people in their group, bringing the total to *ten*. "They called the police, and the police told them of the meeting," she explained. "They insisted on attending. I've just met them myself, and I've told them the stated tone of the meeting. I hope it will be okay." I told her I shared a similar hope!

I immediately went to Bob and advised him of the change. He shrugged. There really wasn't much he could do.

Gradually people came in and sat down, usually nodding to Bob and those in his party. The police were last to arrive.

Caroline and I outlined the ground rules for our discussion. They agreed to follow our direction and instructions for an orderly discussion of the issues. Only one person would speak at a time. Anyone could share in turn or say "pass" in response to a question. Before the end of the meeting, we could decide what was said at the meeting that could be shared in other circles.

The following order was established: We would go around the circle to allow everyone to say their first name and state a particular perspective or concern. Next, we would have a statement from the neighborhood group, followed by an opportunity for Bob to share. Then we would discuss the issues presented.

The first person said that she appreciated the willingness of Bob and his support people to attend such a meeting. Everyone shared their first name and most offered a concern, whether as a parent, a childcare worker, a police officer, a social psychology professor, or the principal of the local elementary school.

Bob gave his name, and he noted that everyone knew why he was here. His parents were concerned and shocked that so many people knew about Bob's presence in such a short time. Joan shared that she had known Bob for more than ten years. She had worked with him in the Sunday school program at a local church.

Sue and another neighbor outlined their questions. We

agreed that they would state their issues without immediate response to the questions. Then Bob would read his prepared statement, which might include some of the issues raised.

The neighbors had a long list of questions. They wanted to know what had happened, what the sentence was, what treatment he had in jail, and what treatment he planned to get now that he was released. They also asked questions about the possibility of re-offending and how he thought the community should respond.

People shifted their attention to Bob, and he read a prepared statement, outlining his offenses in general terms. He expressed appreciation for the constructive method the residents had chosen to follow up their concerns, which he acknowledged as understandable. He reported that he had received some treatment while in prison and had begun to arrange for suitable community-based therapy. He had also set up an accountability system through the pastor of a local church. In that plan, he had daily contact with a person from the church who asked about his faithfulness to his Christian commitment in specific relevant areas.

His biggest concern was his parents. He planned to live with them temporarily, but he wondered if his presence would make it difficult for them to continue to be part of the neighborhood. He acknowledged his offenses and experiences in court and in jail had hurt his parents considerably. "I want to avoid causing them any further pain," he stated.

The others in the room responded with affirmation. One woman said that as a parent, she would want to be supportive of her child no matter what he or she had done. She could understand the parents' role. She added that she did not wish to have the neighbors' concerns with Bob impair his parents' involvement in the neighborhood. Others nodded in agreement.

Through an orderly series of questions and comments, the neighbors obtained more information about what happened, why, and what treatment Bob would get. Bob agreed to talk about the facts of the case, based on what the newspaper had reported at the time of the trial, five years ago. Those present expressed relief when he said that he had previously known all the victims, either through his professional work or as family friends and acquaintances.

At various points the police provided helpful information on the court system and the police role. They affirmed both the neighborhood residents and Bob for working on the issues openly. The police have beeen dealing with increasing demands from communities to provide information on sexual offenders following their release from prison. This puts them in a difficult position of determining how they can fairly and safely balance the rights of all parties.

In an open forum such as this meeting, the police could ensure that residents received correct information from the offender himself—in this case, Bob. It also allowed them to share information while protecting the right to privacy of an accused person.

The area elementary school principal said the school had received calls from parents, and she anticipated that these would increase when the new school year began. Her questions were originally addressed to Bob. However, what followed was a group discussion about how to cope with the issues and provide accurate information without causing undue alarm. One person suggested that the present issue offered a springboard to raise general awareness about sexual abuse. The group wanted to emphasize that in most cases, the abuser is not a stranger, but is someone known and trusted by the child and adults.

The group agreed that those present would talk with other parents in the neighborhood when they asked about information that had been shared at the meeting. If necessary, a public meeting could be organized to process future concerns without Bob present.

As everyone became involved in problem solving, the tension in the room dissipated. Not all the questions were answered. But the participants left with better understanding because of the information provided by Bob and the police. They expressed appreciation for the process and satisfaction with the outcome. By the end of the two-and-a-half hour meeting, the group declared that they had a feeling of accomplishment and were ready to move on.

I, too, had a feeling of accomplishment and hope for the future work that we had to do individually and as a community. This is an example of the reintegration of persons who have offended sexually into a neighborhood. It provides some interesting points for consideration and also raises some questions and concerns.

Strengths of a Neighborhood-Meeting Model

1. It Makes Communication Possible.

It is an effective way to bring together a variety of perspectives in a setting in which information can be given to all parties simultaneously. In volatile neighborhood issues of this sort, concerns tend to escalate based on incomplete and frequently inaccurate information. In the neighborhood meeting, key people, such as the police, can pass on significant information. In that setting, neighbors can feel confident they've heard the truth.

The neighborhood residents were encouraged to share the information with others not at the meeting. They benefited from the chance to raise their concern about protecting neighborhood children. Because of the information they received, there was less likelihood that they would accept inaccurate information or support destructive tactics. The school principal could speak with parents authoritatively, to correct misconceptions and to reassure parents that the school was aware of the issues and was acting to prevent problems. The police were in a better position to answer further inquiries they might receive.

The meeting was just as important for those who were present to support Bob. They were better able to understand the concerns of the neighbors. They could not dismiss the neighbors as overreacting or sensationalist. Frequently those who support "the underdog" tend to be critical of others for their lack of compassion and empathy. By hearing the neighbors' concerns, Bob's supporters were in a better position to support Bob, yet with an awareness of broader issues and perspectives. To be truly supportive of persons who have offended, it is necessary to understand and respect the concerns of others who have been affected by the abuse.

2. It Provides an Opportunity for Education Regarding Sexual Abuse of Children.

As the group discovered, there are many ways to work at the issue of sexual abuse. The meeting educated an attentive audience about sexual abuse in a way that went far beyond the particular factors of a specific situation. Such a process educates each one in the meeting, and this has a ripple effect as they share their information with others.

3. It Shows the Importance of a Quick and Carefully Managed Response.

Neighborhood issues like this begin and spread rapidly. It is crucial to respond quickly. In this case, the neighborhood meeting took place within a week of the initial contact with the agency. Because people are desperate to do something about their strongly held concerns, they often take dramatic steps, such as organizing a neighborhood demonstration in front of the house of a perpetrator.

The facilitators' role is vital. Their task is to hear the concerns and take positive steps, such as contacting the person who has offended. Not all situations work this smoothly. Sometimes more skill and effort is required than was necessary in this instance. Sometimes there is no agreement to meet face-to-face, or such a meeting is not desirable for some reason. There may be ways for a facilitator to defuse a potentially volatile situation by communicating with various "sides" of the issue. The facilitators would attempt to mediate some of the concerns raised by the parties.

In this example, the various parties expressed considerable goodwill prior to the meeting. Hence, the facilitators did not have to use interventions to reduce hostility or address concerns for safety. In other cases, such interventions would be necessary.

4. It Is an Action to Prevent a Problem Rather Than Waiting to React to a Problem.

Sue's initial phone call allowed many individuals to participate in the response. By providing the opportunity for people to engage in constructive problem solving, we reduced the likelihood of harmful words or actions.

I wish we could take more steps to prevent problems. That might mean establishing contact with the person who offended before his release from prison. Such a plan would involve various community support persons and area residents in planning with the inmate how best to facilitate the return to his or her home community.[2]

5. It Is Restorative Justice at Work.

There is a tremendous amount of hurt and pain in our families, neighborhoods, and churches. In this situation, we offered information and healing. People could learn and change their views without jeopardizing the safety of potential victims. We tried to deal restoratively with a specific situation. We included a wide range of viewpoints on the issue and on potential solutions. We gave the people involved the authority and skills to resolve the questions. Restorative justice was at work.

Concerns That Must Be Raised

There can be other concerns with this approach that should be discussed.

1. Sharing of True Feelings Could Be Inhibited.

When the person who has offended is present, people may find it awkward to share what they are really thinking and feeling. Several times people said: "Nothing personal, but from what I've heard about sex offenders . . ." Facilitators need repeatedly to give permission for participants to express differing views and to state that the purpose of the meeting is to share honestly, not necessarily to agree on all points.

2. Previously Held Stereotypes Could Be Confirmed.

In the meeting I described, Bob was personable, calm in conversation, and quite able to express his point of view and hear others' concerns. Another offender might more closely portray a stereotypical "sex offender" in his appearance and actions. Then the concerned neighbors might have their fears confirmed.

Similarly, the person who has offended may decline to share information in response to a question, perhaps for legitimate but unknown reasons. The neighbors may then react with suspicion and fear, which would obviously affect the productiveness of the meeting. The facilitators should simultaneously respect each member's privacy and encourage everyone to be as forthright as possible.

As the facilitators make arrangements, they will gain a sense of how the meeting will proceed. The facilitators should guard against unrealistic expectations. If the person who offended appears evasive in the meeting, or even worse, fails to appear, others might harden their attitudes.

3. Appropriate Follow-Up Is Important.

While all parties may have agreed to have one meeting, the facilitators may need to follow up, to ensure that further issues or concerns will be processed. This may mean that if any concerns arise in the neighborhood, they will be addressed directly to the ex-offender or a designated representative. It may be necessary to arrange more meetings of the key parties to ensure that the agreed-upon arrangements are satisfying the stated concerns.

A meeting as described here is only the first step in helping a community accept an important fact: people who have offended, been convicted, and imprisoned do return to live in neighborhoods, sooner or later. Most of them do not die in prison. Longer-term follow-up is essential; we cannot ignore this task.

Case 2: Victim-Offender Dialogues

Lorraine wanted to dialogue with someone who had committed offenses against several people (other than herself). Her search led her to Esther, who contacted me. Esther was a staff person for a church relief agency. Here are excerpts from Lorraine's initial conversation with me and from her journal:

Lorraine: I have a vision. Someday I want to tell my story to an audience that also listens to a perpetrator telling his story. Then when we have finished, we would stand together before God in a reconciled sort of way, maybe even hand in hand.

When I think of the church and the patriarchal power structure, I think that it could change to become a people-oriented organization by the efforts of women and men who get together to dismantle and then rebuild it. This will insure that the uneven power-control structure of the past is not repeated.

I think of the victim-offender struggle in much the same way. In a few years, as women reclaim their voice, more and more perpetrators of sexual abuse will surface, and we all will have to find a way to be with each other. So journeying with a perpetrator will in some measure be a tearing down and rebuilding of relationships, a learning to be with each other.

I'm aware that this could be a very hard journey. I am not afraid to hurt. I have found out that if my hurting is related to my healing, then when I hurt, I am healing. Even as I am writing now, I am becoming very scared. My stomach wants to move up into my chest. It wants to share its ache with my whole body—pushing up, I suppose, to shut up my voice as well.

* * * * * * * * *

Lorraine: I promise you, body, that I will take good care of you. I will hold you when you hurt, and speak and write the truth as it happens. I will find good people who will help me through this.

Lord Jesus, I ask that you go with me. I fear the lions

and their gnashing teeth, but I feel somewhere in my heart that the lions are really lambs. Hurting lambs, as I am. Besides, I am a woman lioness, am I not? I can protect the little girl inside me and face and embrace all of life.

Lord Jesus, I can do it! I can face anything. Even as I am writing this, though, I am becoming increasingly scared.

Lorraine, why do you do these things? Why do you get frightened and do what you do?

* * * * * * * * * *

Lorraine: This journey isn't just about me. It is also about my perpetrator. How else could I understand and continue my healing without being with and loving one who was like my father? I know, whoever you are, I will hate you, but I wonder if we can walk long enough and hard enough, that I can love you as well.

* * * * * * * * * *

Lorraine: Lord, I want to try this. With fear and trepidation, I want to move forward, and I want to finish my journey truly loving. Loving myself and those who hurt me. I believe there is much we can learn from each other. Maybe if I could know that you hear me, I can then hear you too. We don't have to do this alone, you know. There are people out there who will walk with us. I'm sure we can find them.

* * * * * * * * * *

Lorraine's courage and deep faith commitment were evident in what she had written. I wanted to meet Lorraine and explore her hopes for a journey toward restoration. Esther and I arranged a meeting where Lorraine shared her wishes, concerns, and boundaries. These formed the framework for a series of dialogues with Steve.

Wishes

Lorraine: As persons, we are created in God's own image and called into right relationship with God, self, and others. Our bodily lives are affirmed (1 Cor. 3:16-17).

It is my wish to journey with a perpetrator, to continue work on my healing journey. I want to be with someone who can dialogue on different levels—spiritual, emotional, and intellectual. This person should be strong enough to be able to be with me in my anger and to continue the journey if things get tough. Face-to-face, we should be able to express feelings, share impressions, and interact with care and sensitivity.

I want to talk about my abuse and my journey thus far.

I wish to be able to explore the journey of this partner. This person must be willing to take risks with himself within this relationship. It will be important to wrestle with anger, shame, denial, and the process of recovery, as well as with patterns that contribute to this type of behavior, both for myself and the person with whom I journey.

It is important that we speak the truth as much as we are able.

Power and authority issues will need to be addressed, as well as other theological issues. At times I might want to grapple with scriptural texts as they relate to abuse.

The person should be a male who is at least thirty-five years of age.

Concerns

Lorraine: Although I feel I am able to take care of myself, I am also aware that this journey could revictimize me. This scares me a little.

I am concerned for my physical safety.

I am concerned about the issue of money. I will need a therapist to journey with me, and I am not sure how long I will be able to continue paying for this. I go to school and do not work for pay, so my finances are limited.

I need to know that the person I am partnered with has a place to go to debrief. Maybe even a support group to help with the difficult issues.

I am concerned about my right to express my feelings. This is very important to me and will be a definite part of this relationship. I will need to know that this person respects my process for healing and my timetable for recovery. When I say, "no," or "wait," I cannot be pushed to carry on.

I am concerned about the connection between spirituality and sexuality and how this will manifest itself in this relationship. Therefore, I need help in setting clear boundaries. I would like clear expectations from the person I am partnered with. Perhaps we need to agree on boundary items in a contractual fashion.

I would like boundary issues to be discussed between him and me, but in the presence of Esther and Mark.

Selecting a Partner

Based on the extensive information Lorraine provided, I considered who might be a suitable dialogue partner. I felt some fear about proceeding. I felt inspired by Lorraine's explanation of her hopes and fears, and I did not want to contribute to a harmful outcome, or re-victimization, as she called it.

I felt confident in approaching Steve. His healing journey had extended over four years. More significantly, I had confidence in the depth of his search and his growing self-awareness. Equally valuable, I felt he most closely shared the kind of spiritual journey that Lorraine had identified as significant for her. He sought to integrate his spiritual journey as part of his growth and change.

As I shared Lorraine's wishes and concerns with Steve, he responded sensitively and expressed the deep respect he felt for her interest in pursuing this dialogue. He immediately saw ways that this could be beneficial in furthering and deepening his own understanding and growth. Perhaps it would help him to understand better the pain of his own daughter whom he had abused. I found confirmation for my sense that he would be a good partner for Lorraine.

After Steve agreed to participate, Steve, Lorraine, Esther, and I held an initial meeting. We decided how to set up the dialogue, and we discussed boundary issues. Lorraine shared a statement on what setting boundaries meant for her.

Boundaries

Lorraine: I have a need to create a safe place for meeting this person. I want to meet in public places, or if we're in a closed room, we need to be in a building where other people are present. No meeting in my house or his house. No car rides or desolate meeting places.

I would like it if there is no exchange of money. Coffee maybe, but nothing else. If we eat together, we pay our own bills. Alcohol should not be consumed by either of us before or during our meetings. The sessions should probably be one to one and a half hours, unless we agree on something else ahead of time.

Dual relationships[3] shall not be established during the time we are journeying.

No sexual contact or sexualized behavior will be allowed in this relationship. We will learn to show our connection with each other in different ways. No discussion of my personal sexual relationship with my spouse.

My marriage must be preserved at all costs. If problems arise in the marriage that seem too difficult to resolve with this relationship in the wings, and if solutions cannot be found, I will end this relationship.

Both agreed to these arrangements at that initial meeting and made a commitment that there would not be direct dialogue between Steve and Lorraine except at their meetings. They would handle any arrangements, cancellations, or changes in meetings through Esther or me. This provided additional control to avoid intrusions. (More than a year after this first meeting, they shared their telephone numbers so they could reschedule meeting times or dates.)

First Dialogue

I remember that first meeting well. Esther and I felt somewhat nervous and uncertain, and so did Lorraine and Steve. Yet Lorraine and Steve engaged in forthright and open conversation. Following the session, I asked Steve how he felt. He had anticipated what was ahead and felt nervous about how it would work out.

Lorraine shared journal excerpts written after the initial meeting.

Lorraine: I was quite nervous at first. I had been thinking about this meeting during the day. I wondered if I would hate Steve the minute I saw him. Whenever I think of my dad, I get angry and defensive. But this wasn't the case. I was able to welcome him and thank him for considering taking this journey with me.

We first talked about how we were feeling. All four of us were a little nervous. I felt very vulnerable during the meeting. Esther said afterward that I looked and spoke with control, but I was not feeling controlled inside.

I felt strange when we read over the boundaries I had set. I almost felt as if I was accusing him before we even started. I wonder if other survivors feel this. The need to please outweighs the need for protection. Was there always this need to please my father even though I hated him?

Maybe the need to please came before the hate. Was this how I received strokes as a child? If only I could please them, then they would see how important I was. In doing this, I must have lost the ability or knowledge to please myself. This was probably some of the confusion I experienced while becoming an adult. How could I please myself and others too? For attention, I chose to please others. It is only through my healing journey that I finally turned around and listened to the still voice that pleases *me*.

So how do I connect that with last night? There was a time at the meeting when I felt safe enough to offer Steve my telephone number. But I chose not to trust. I hope by choosing this I do not interrupt the process. For once in my life, I am going to choose not to trust. Trust is a funny thing, isn't it? It has always been an issue for me.

Counselor: Lorraine, you have a right to set your own boundaries, and a right to remain safe. You need to choose what boundaries to put in place and when. First find out what you need and then be specific, not fluid, with setting those boundaries.

Lorraine: So to be clear, I will not trust Steve with my safety. Although I want to create a relationship with him, it will have to be a relationship that has strong and not fluid boundaries. This is okay. I will trust him, though, to the extent of sharing my journey.

I will trust that God is at the head of this. I trust that this is a process that is in place to facilitate healing for both of us, and I will trust the process. This scares me a bit, because I don't want to be hurt again, but I had a real sense last night that Steve does not want to hurt me. He actually wants to aid in my healing. In so doing, it might give him a chance to let go of some of the hurt he has caused others.

I felt heard by Steve last night. I also felt some of his journey. When he said he has learned some amazing things, I could identify with this. My road too has been very rocky. It has been extremely hard, but the most amazing things have happened.

I also felt that Steve's Christian walk is important to him. My spirituality is very important to me also. I am excited to be able to share this part of my journey with him. I love to share my spirituality. Last night as we talked, I felt as if I was on holy ground. It felt like a sacred meeting. Thank you, Jesus, for being there with us.

I really liked the way Steve was not afraid to look me in the eye when we spoke, or even when I was talking about boundaries. This helped me feel connected to him in some way.

On the way home, I was able to discuss with my friend Heather the positive things that happened. When I got home, my husband met me at the door, and I started to cry. The impact of the whole thing hit me. I'm going to share my story with a perpetrator, and I'm going to have to hear his story. This could be a very painful experience for me. But I already knew that, didn't I? I knew this would be hard but rewarding.

I tossed and turned all night. The feeling of vulnerability rarely left me. I awoke tired and almost fell asleep twice at work today. So now I am going to go to bed to have a good sleep.

Thank you, Lord, for Steve, for his sensitivity, his caring and sharing attitude. Be with him as we continue. Help us to be honest and open with each other, and help us to deal with abuse issues. I do not want to be revictimized, nor do I want to victimize. Lord, be with me. Lord, be with us!

That was the beginning. Steve and Lorraine met on their own within the guidelines outlined. After several meetings, Esther and I met with them to check how things were going. Then I got periodic updates from Steve. Esther got updates from Lorraine and served as a communication link. The only deviation from the guidelines was the length of each meeting. The suggested time of sixty to ninety minutes was generally stretched to two hours or more.

After twelve sessions, the four of us met to review what had been done. I sensed the difference in atmosphere from our first meeting. These were two people who had shared deeply. They were ready with many observations. I summarized some themes from that discussion under the following headings.

Telling Their Stories

They began their dialogues by telling their stories to each other. Steve described his reaction to hearing Lorraine's story.

> *Steve:* What struck me about your story, Lorraine, was the amount of pain, confusion, and deep hurt you experienced. I had some understanding of it before, but hearing it so vividly drove it home a lot more. Especially the part where you described how you would curl up in a ball at night. I'll never forget that session. That reinforced a lot of things for me.
>
> I found myself wanting to be careful—was I respecting your boundaries? At first I was aware of this in the little things, like who walked out of the room first, and who turned off the lights. Now I'm much more comfortable with how we relate to each other.

A few days after Lorraine shared her story, she asked Esther to make sure Steve was all right. Lorraine had sensed the deep impact her story had on him. Steve coped with his intense feelings about Lorraine's story by driving around in his car for a while after their meeting and talking with a close friend.

Steve was surprised that Lorraine had been able to hear the specifics of his offending.

Steve: You haven't shut me out, in spite of what I've done.

Lorraine: I can't understand why I don't hate you. We said at the beginning that you're not my father. I really want to understand you, and if I shut you down, I never will be able to understand you.

Lorraine wrote about sharing her story with Steve.

Lorraine: Last night I shared parts of my story with Steve. I was not able to look him in the eye the way he looked me in the eye when he told his story. I wonder what that was all about. I wanted to trust him, but we were alone. It wasn't the same as talking to my friends or my husband. He was a guy, and I was talking about intimate things. I felt some shame.

I felt very full sometimes. Even the room felt very full for me. Was the Spirit there? I am sure. But I couldn't look him in the eye. This bothered me a great deal. It is as if I didn't have control. He trusted me with his story. He shared himself openly, and I couldn't. I told my story, my truth, but I couldn't open myself. Was I protecting me or him?

I didn't want to see his pain. I didn't want to fully connect. I detached a bit from him. Is this a good thing? I don't want this [relationship] to be this way all the time. I need to stay attached as I speak my truth. I need to feel that he hears my pain.

I was thankful for the silences that he allowed. He didn't rush me. These silences were very loud for me. I was so full inside. The fullness wasn't anger, though. Let's see: what was it? It was full and thick like a marshmallow. Was there someone with me in that thickness? It felt sacred. Many things feel sacred to me.

It was very difficult for Lorraine to hear Steve talk in detail about when he sexually abused his daughter.

Lorraine: I really feel pain when we talk about your daughter Beth and what you did to her. I still have trouble hearing that. Usually when I touch my pain, it feels so sacred to me, but this doesn't; it still feels hard and unfinished. It has not yet integrated the way my other pain has.

Sometimes people give the impression, either clearly stated or unspoken, that by talking things through, we can find an acceptable explanation for the sexual abuse. This questionable assumption was explored by Lorraine.

> *Lorraine:* What I found really hard listening to your story, Steve, was that when you talk about the abusive behavior, I just don't understand. Something tells me that even after all you've said to me about your story and with the compassion I feel for the pain you've suffered, it still doesn't allow me to say, "You had a right to do what you did," or "I can see now how it happened."

The definitive answer always seems elusive. More healing is done in searching for an answer than in actually finding a final answer.

> *Steve:* I think I've come to realize that no reason or explanation is good enough.

Spiritual Relationship

As I have gotten to know Lorraine and Steve, I am impressed by their deep faith, a resource that both have treasured and used in their separate healing journeys. This book has shared comments about religious expectations and demands that were not helpful. The church fosters and undergirds faith, which has great potential as a healing resource and as a catalyst to change judgmental attitudes.

As the two discussed their relationship with God, they learned of their differences. Steve found this challenging.

> *Steve:* For me, it was refreshing to hear a different point of view on spirituality. I think after hearing your story, Lorraine, I long to be spiritually connected the way you are. My spirituality is more "head knowledge" and less personal than what I have heard you describe from your journey.

Lorraine recorded her early impressions in her journal:

Lorraine: We talked about God tonight. Steve says that he has more of a relationship with Jesus now than he ever had before. I would like to explore this with him a bit more. I am very cautious, though. Religion can be used as a crutch or as "something to make you feel good about yourself." So, is it that I don't want him to feel good about himself?

He has come so far in his healing that he has somehow accepted that he is who he is. He doesn't seem to be proud of the abuse he has perpetrated on others, but he seems to have a grounded sense of himself. We need to explore this more.

Touchstones

I have a collection of rocks that I picked up at various beaches in years past. I don't remember where I picked up these interesting stones, but I do have memories attached to them. There is a smooth, shiny rock that brings a feeling of well-being and warmth. Another rock is rough and jagged and reminds me of cold and unrelenting waves washing against the shore. These and other rocks are touchstones for me, connecting me to the moods and emotions I feel at different times. They can become reference points to ground me in the variety of experiences that are a part of my past.

When charting a healing journey, reference points or touchstones along the way can provide clear direction. The touchstones for survivors and those who have offended will be different, shaped by experiences and responses.

A touchstone can become a heavy weight that holds back or drags down. The person who has offended will have a tendency to want to quickly put the abuse in the past and move on. Because the abuse is deeply significant, the person who moves on too quickly loses connection with an important part of himself. One who offends may select touchstones that reinforce previously learned patterns of minimization and denial, and that is not good. He needs touchstones that remind him of his dawning sense of responsibility.

It is worthwhile to maintain symbols and rituals that allow people to connect with what has happened. For survivors, touchstones also become memorable reference points in a healing journey. A person who has experienced the devastation of sexual abuse will probably never be completely healed from its effect. While we may encourage them to move on, they need reference points that connect them to the pain they suffered, so they can own that, too.

On one hand, individuals whose identity is almost totally shaped by the abuse may experience it as a heavy weight to be dragged along. On the other hand, persons who minimize or deny its impact will also be blocked in their healing.

People who have offended usually want to move on more quickly than survivors or others. This came up in the discussion with Steve and Lorraine. Lorraine wanted to hear not only about "victories," but also about the struggles.

> *Lorraine:* When I hear you talking about your victories and how free you feel, then I want to know where your struggle is and if you are really still continuing your journey on your own healing. My philosophy is that you can't have "resurrection" without "Good Friday," and if I keep hearing about resurrection, I think about denial.

> *Steve:* When I look back on what I've done, I felt an emotional void. I could not be free to be who I was, to express how I was hurting. Learning to be myself is an ongoing process. If I stop that learning, then, yes, I can revert to my old ways of seeking emotional satisfaction through sexual expression. But my journey is now a constant walk of satisfying my emotional self, and I'm learning to do it spiritually as well.

Steve listed warning signals or touchstones that he has found important to attend to on an ongoing basis.

> If I'm feeling myself slide or having feelings of worthlessness, I know I need to pay attention to that. At other times, I feel as if I'm lost or spinning my wheels; that's a danger

signal as well. If I start to masturbate a lot or experience a lot of stress, that's another danger signal.

The survivor and the initiator of sexual abuse both feel the pain and anguish surrounding sexual abuse and its aftermath. We should not try to compare the suffering of persons but provide touchstones for each person to do his or her work. Lorraine considered this in her journal.

Lorraine: My father hurt me when I was a little girl, and for many years I held a lot of anger and hatred for him. Now I meet Steve, who is a perpetrator, but who is willing to talk to me about it. We are talking about important things and at a wonderful level. Although this scares me a little, I want to continue being with these things and working through more of them.

A perpetrator hurt me, and here I am, later in life, enjoying a relationship with a perpetrator. I am touched that other people come full circle in their journeys for healing. God, is this the way of the universe? If we allow life to happen to us, then we will heal. Is this part of the circle? We eat plants, then die and become food for the plants. We are hurt, and in order to heal, we come to a new understanding by knowing someone who also hurt.

This feels very complicated to me, yet also very spiritual. My relationship with Steve feels very spiritual, very universal, and it seems to be fitting into the natural unfolding of my journey. God creates this way. Thank you, God. Thank you to my husband for being who you are and trusting this relationship with Steve. Thank you, Steve, for being a part of my healing journey. Thank you, Lorraine, for allowing your life to unfold as it does, and [as it] should.

Concluding Observations

I want to outline observations for further consideration and discussion.

1. Applying This Dialogue Experience to Others

I admire and appreciate the courage and pioneering spirit that Steve and Lorraine showed in undertaking this journey.

The healing and growth that had already occurred in both their lives contributed positively to the success of this healing journey. I believe their experience in such dialogue is not unique.

My experience with survivors and those who have offended has given me a profound sense of optimism and hope. I count on the God-given resilience of the human spirit and the search for wholeness and healing. I feel there can be broader applications within the boundaries that were present in this case, which ensured the safety and self-determination of participants.

2. Dialogue Impacted from Not Knowing Each Other

In this instance, two people shared deeply concerning one aspect of their lives in which there was a common theme, sexual abuse. Because they did not know each other previously, they could focus on the narrow issue of sexual abuse without addressing many other factors. That would be impossible if, for example, a father met with a daughter whom he had sexually abused many years earlier.

Steve reported that this provided him with valuable learning for dialogue with the daughter he had abused, if his victim wanted that in the future.

3. Accounting for Personal and Gender Differences in Working on Issues

It can be difficult to sort out individual responses in a dialogue such as the one outlined above. What responses from victim and offender are related to their personality traits? What are related to their gender? Which responses does one usually get from a survivor or from someone who offended? I have no answers, but simply offer the question.

4. Reacting to Common Themes Shared by Survivors and Offenders

In this book, we recognize many links between the healing journeys of survivors and those who offend. Having similar issues does not mean that their journeys are the same. It is useful to identify common things in their experiences, but we must remember that the fundamental distinction between the abuser and the abused cannot be erased. To even try such a thing would be serious injustice to all parties.

Sexual abuse is always a fundamental betrayal of the trust that a vulnerable person has in a more powerful person. We must not permit the discussion of common features to cloud our awareness of this difference between victim and the one who offends. On the other hand, we can take steps to allow those who have offended to move on in their healing journey.

5. Facilitating Such a Dialogue

I am frequently awed by the trust and faith that survivors and those who have offended place in me to assist in their healing. With the trust comes the obligation to be responsible and sensitive toward the persons involved. No one can guarantee that such a dialogue will be uplifting and helpful. Yet one can provide reasonable safety for persons wanting to test new ways of healing. Facilitators should acknowledge and uphold this sacred trust.

Case 3: Ounce of Prevention Workshop

The Ounce of Prevention Workshop is an annual gathering of persons affected by and interested in sexual abuse and how it can be prevented. It was built on a graduate student project on the prevention of child sexual abuse and has continued on an annual basis for the past five years. The planning and presentations for this event, open to the community, are done by men and women who have been involved in the agency's groups for survivors, offenders, or partners, and by other community volunteers.

Melissa Miller attended the Friday evening and all-day Saturday sessions and wrote the following account:[4]

I attended the Ounce of Prevention [Workshop] this past October and was awed by the experience. The first thing I noticed was the pain. Those were people who had endured some of the deepest hurts of life, and it showed in their eyes and the way they carried their bodies.

Second, I noticed their sensitivity and compassion. Even when difficult things were being said, they listened carefully to each other and disagreed respectfully, accepting each one's perspective.

Then I noticed their courage and power, the way they used their voices and their gifts. Trevor is a young man in his mid-twenties who suffers from multiple personality disorder. He participated in a panel discussion, telling the story of his healing from sexual abuse by many people. The abuse started with his mother when he was three or four.

As he looked out at us, Trevor's eyes were still clouded with pain and confusion about the horrendous things he had suffered. He also had a warm and engaging presence, a sweet smile, and an ability to articulate his healing. I marvel at his bravery.

The same with Tom, who sat beside Trevor. Tom spoke of the harm he had done by abusing his daughter. He named one of the consequences of his actions, that she does not want to be around him, and he recognizes how much he has lost.

Kelly, on the same panel, talked about her abuse by a family friend when she was a young teenager and how difficult it has been for her to deal with the guilt she feels. "I was just coming into a time of sexual awakening," she said, "and he exploited that. But because of my developing sexuality, I tended to blame myself for the abuse."

Shauna was a social worker who described how she became involved and worked in the field of sexual abuse for many years, always wondering about her interest and motivation. "When I went home this summer," she said, "I found out. It's because of all these dynamics in my family that are just under the surface, but I hadn't named them."

Shauna also gently voiced her belief that the groupings separating survivors from offenders and from the rest of us are harmful, and that we need to find ways to dissolve the lines, so we can all work together to make our communities sexually healthy places. Others on the panel and in the audience nodded.

Together we watched an energizing drama, written by one of the volunteers who is a former offender. We observed a group of actors portraying a family where there were some danger signals about sexual inappropriateness. Then the audience instructed members of the drama troupe how to play their parts differently so that the abuse would not happen.

And that's it in a nutshell, isn't it? The community needs to be so involved in each other's lives that we can say, "Live in such a way that sexual abuse does not happen. Develop healthy sexuality. Protect children. Don't sexualize the relationship you have with the less-powerful person in your care. Recognize where you are vulnerable, and get your intimacy needs met in ways that do not harm others."

We have the Ounce of Prevention weekends because many individuals have labored long and hard to create a climate where people can meet. Survivors have told their stories, and through many hours of group participation, individual therapy, and sheer gritty work, they found healing. Persons who have offended have in similar formats examined their own offenses, taken responsibility for their harmful actions, changed their abusive ways, sought to understand the reasons for their offending, and explored ways to give something back to the community. This process takes years.

Family members have opened their own hearts to journeying with their loved ones and learning about sexual abuse and about healing. Counselors and pastors have invested much emotional energy in supporting individuals as they heal. I want to be clear that an event like Ounce of Prevention is possible only after much healing.

Still, it is possible, and it does exist in our world. Perhaps Ounce of Prevention may point you to some concrete dreams of where we might go as we heal from sexual abuse, as it does for me.

We ended our time at Ounce of Prevention by tossing an unrolling ball of string back and forth, and naming our feelings, hopes, and struggles. Each declared that he or she was brave, happy, confused, angry, hurting, broken, healing, or hopeful. We held onto the string and wrapped ourselves in a web that reminded us of our connections.

In my pocket now I carry the piece of string that I brought away from Ounce of Prevention. It reminds me of my ties to members of my community who have direct experience with sexual abuse, and that we are all trying to change so our communities are safe and healthy. May you also find such a web of connection as you work for change and healing in your life, your family, your church, and your community.

14

A Family
Eight Years Later

This chapter summarizes important factors we need to address in dealing with sexual abuse.

As in earlier parts of the book, I asked others to help me. In this case, a family reflects on their experiences eight years after a revelation of sexual abuse: Dave, husband and father; Joanne, wife and mother; and their two daughters, Sandy and Carol. Dave was charged by police after Sandy, then an adolescent, informed her teacher that Dave had been sexually abusing her over an extended period. Considerable upheaval followed.

We sat in the living room of their home. As we began to talk, the reality of the abuse seemed remote as Sandy chatted excitedly about plans for her wedding to a man she had met at Bible college. The conversation that followed helped to bridge the gap between those contrasting pictures. The family shared about the eight intervening years and the ways they have dealt with the abuse, which they acknowledge still significantly affects their lives.

> *Joanne:* I wonder whether the struggles we have as a family are a result of the abuse, or whether the struggles are ones that every family goes through typically at this point in their life cycle; for example, kids pulling in different directions, midlife crisis, unemployment, serious illness, marital

issues. I also wonder if the commitment to see it through is as a result of the abuse or something else.

I appreciate the family's willingness to share their journey. I respect and admire their dedication and resilience. They state their feelings and impressions clearly. I hope readers will listen to the depth of their experiences, rather than limiting themselves to the narrow question of whether the family remained together. While this family is intact, I do not offer their experiences as the standard for other families. In many families, it is not possible or desirable for a family unit to be re-constituted after the revelation of abuse. People must have a sense of choice and autonomy, and feel control over their destiny as much as possible.

In many current cases, we cope with sexual abuse that occurred many years ago. So we must peel back layers of hurt added to the initial hurt. This family's story provides hope that if issues are dealt with closer to the time of the abuse, it is easier to handle them wholistically and thoroughly. While they still need to discuss the abuse, the family members report a clear sense of movement.

> *Joanne:* There has never been a time in the past eight years that this topic was unapproachable or taboo for our family. As each of the girls has hit different stages and phases in their lives, this gets reworked. When Carol hit the age Sandy had been at the time of the disclosure, there were some struggles. As we've gone through different stages, we have had to rework and renegotiate who we are as a family.

The Wrongdoer Taking Responsibility

Frequently when I speak with survivors of sexual abuse, I am struck by the intense rage they feel because the wrongdoer refuses to acknowledge the acts. This denial is often bolstered by others who do not wish to hear about it. To encourage persons who offend to take responsibility for their actions, we must provide an environment that encourages such a step and supports it.

> *Sandy:* One important factor for me being able to work through this whole thing was that right from square one, Dad admitted what he had done, and he took full responsibility for it. That made it ten times easier for me. Being able to resolve issues with Dad and eventually accept Dad back into the family was so much easier because Dad said, "It was wrong, and it's not your fault."

Often the accused person does not accept responsibility quickly and completely. I asked Dave why he took responsibility so readily and without minimizing.

> *Dave:* I knew while the abuse was going on that it was wrong. But it was almost like I couldn't stop myself. One of my biggest fears was that if I told [my wife], then it would be "game over," end of the family, and I didn't really want that. I knew in myself that I had a lot of problems to deal with, but I didn't know how to get started.
>
> The disclosure was really the point that allowed me to break free and say, "Let's look at the issues." At that point there was nothing to gain by hiding it. I can't see what lying would do at that point except just cover up more secrets.
>
> For me, the disclosure was the best thing that ever happened, because I certainly look at life in a much different way and am able to look at life more confidently.

Recognizing the Issue of Trust

Trust does not automatically follow once the individual accepts responsibility.

> *Sandy:* Dad really blew it, and he had to work over a period of time with all of us to regain our trust and for us to feel confident that he was never going to do this again.

The trust issue needed to be processed with Sandy and her sister, Carol. It was also a real issue for Joanne, who had to decide whether to continue the marriage. She states clearly that her primary aim was to protect her children. The future of the marriage relationship was much in doubt.

Joanne: In the process of Dave and me renegotiating what we were going to be, if indeed we were going to be [a couple] at all, the whole issue of trust was a really major one. I didn't trust anything he said. Nothing! That is something that has come back in little steps.

I remember saying to Dave at one of our many meetings, "If you don't like the fact that I'm going to be checking up on you when you're back in the family, then you might as well leave now. I'm going to be checking regularly with both my daughters. If you aren't prepared for the process of earning some trust back, then you can leave, and this is it."

It was going to have to be a very slow process, because I felt that everything Dave and I had previously built was gone.

The issue of trust had a different twist a number of years later, when Dave and Joanne had difficulty trusting Sandy. She chose questionable friends and became involved with alcohol and drugs. Her family could not rely on her. I inquired if there was a connection.

Sandy: Originally it was Dad who lost my trust because of the abuse. Then I guess as a way of retaliating, I ended up doing a lot of really stupid stuff and breaking my parents' trust.

Dave: As Sandy says, I had to earn her trust back. I think that is what change is all about, because when she says something to me, I know her word is good, and at that basic level it's more than trust.

Sandy: It's respect, I think.

Family Struggles

The disclosure set off a serious crisis for the family and led to many conflicts as the family attempted to cope. Sandy described her fear immediately following the disclosure.

After the whole thing had blown up, I was scared stiff that Dad would be really angry with me because he was arrested, [involving] police, courts, and everything else. I really didn't want to deal with Dad right after it first happened.

She remembers her fears as she approached her home, after spending those first hours with child protection services and the police.

Sandy: I was scared to go home, but I didn't want to go into foster care. When I came home, the first thing Mom did was meet me at the door and give me a great big hug. She said, "I'm sorry this happened, I believe you, and it's not your fault." I knew then that Mom was very supportive of me, and that was very helpful.

When the family began to face the sexual abuse issues in treatment, there were many dynamics to consider. Despite efforts to include Carol, the "nonaffected" family member, she remembers the experience this way:

Carol: I always felt the counselor treated me like a kid, and I was never included in any of the family stuff. I hated it. Like here's the mom and dad, and things have to be worked out between them, and between Sandy and Dad, and Sandy and Mom. But I'm just a kid.

Sandy: Nine times out of ten, Carol was sent to play with the toys in the waiting room. Other times she was at the session, but she wasn't really *in it.*

Family members were repeatedly asked whether they would work at the issues as parts of a family unit.

Joanne: I think we all had different points in time when we wondered if we wanted to stay together. Whether or not it would be a reality was something we worked at every single day. At first I had no interest in being together. I was so angry over what had happened.

There have been blocks of time when family members were separated. For more than a year after the initial disclosure, Dave did not live with the family. Sandy also lived apart from the family several times and went to Bible college.

Sandy: My year at Bible college was really good because it allowed me the transition time to do some growing up, and it allowed the family to deal with me being gone. It let me come back as a different person than when I went away.

When she returned from Bible college, she chose to live at home. Family members describe that family time as the most stable.

During our conversation, the family frequently spoke about the tentativeness of their family unit and the series of crises with which they have coped. They have worked through a series of issues over the past eight years. One of the most significant was Joanne's life-threatening illness. For Sandy, that put some things in sharper focus.

When Mom, who had always been the strong one, became very sick and was in a coma, it was the most terrifying thing that ever happened to Carol and me. It far exceeded the issues surrounding the sexual abuse disclosure. I don't mean to minimize it, but that life-threatening illness was terrifying. It's like coming head-to-head with mortality. Mom and Dad aren't going to be around forever, and our family had been fighting a lot before then.

From listening to the family talk, I gained the clear impression that their various trials and frayed ends had been woven like a fabric to create stronger individuals and a stronger family. As they planned for Sandy's marriage, they commented on the relative calm and stability that they feel as their lives move toward a brighter future.

Sandy: It feels like we're at a landmark now as a family for how far we've come. We're not where we were at the time of the abuse. It feels like we've gone from one crisis to another, and now finally we've slowed down.

Church and Faith

Joanne: God is with us in the muck of our lives.

Their deep faith commitment was a clear source of strength and renewal. They encouraged churches to offer practical support in place of platitudes.

Dave: I think the church's role is important. However, the church does an offender a disservice by not allowing him to go into the depths of his own soul because that is very necessary for healing. The church has a tendency to serve up platitudes like "Jesus saves," and "grace is freely given." Both of these are true. But each of us has to struggle in the real depths of our core with that dismal reality.

Joanne: I see the difference this way. Do you bail someone out? Or do you go and sit with them in the depth of their pain, as they realize what they have done? Or do you say, "We'll make it better. God forgives." I think when others are able to sit in the presence of that pain, then God is present.

Dave: One of the most important images in the Bible for me is Jesus hanging on the cross and saying, "My God, my God, why have you forsaken me." It was only out of that anguish that I was able to rise again. I had to be there because there were times when I was overwhelmed by the sheer fact of what I had done—this was a child! The horror hit me.

I think that deep pain is something an offender needs to go through. That's why we don't do them any favors by shielding them from going through that pain. Unless they do, they won't fundamentally change. If they're told, "It's okay; it's just something that happened," they won't truly acknowledge the harm they have caused. It's *not* just something that happened.

I had to rediscover who I was. I didn't like who I was. But I also had to come to the place where I could accept who I was and who I could become. This is where the church can be a support, in those times of deep struggle. I think there's a big difference between offering platitudes and providing support.

They offered examples of practical support from people in the church. There were meals and short-term accommodation for Dave, pastors who spent hours waiting in boring courtroom areas, and an assistant pastor who supported in a special way.

Sandy: She used to take me out for a milkshake. She treated me like an equal, with no sense of, "Oh, you're a *victim*." She was cool.

Remembering, Yet Moving On

Throughout our conversation, they recalled various symbols that reminded family members of past events. They showed me a birthday card for Sandy with a blank where Dave's name would have been. She got it shortly after the disclosure. On her computer disk, Carol still has a story she wrote about her trouble forgiving her sister.

Carol: And remember, Dad, the letter you sent to me when you were in jail? It said, "You have a lot of courage, Carol, and I still love you." It still makes me cry when I think about it. I still have that letter. I used to keep it in my Bible, but I was afraid my friends might find it and ask questions.

They also showed me a hood ornament from their old car. Though they no longer used the car, the hood ornament reminded them of the many trips family members took to meetings during the first six months—an average of one a day.

Conclusion of Family Session

As we concluded our discussion, I felt hopeful. The people in this family, like those in the Book Reference Group and many others, have renewed my optimism for the resilience of the human spirit. People must change and they can. Courageous people have taken risks to heal and grow, and to conquer lurking demons. They point the direction for us. May all of us in our own way follow their example.

15

Epilogue

The story is told of a community that lived by a river. Often a child would be caught in the current, and the somebody would rescue them from the river downstream. Many caring people worked valiantly to save the children's lives and nurture them back to health. In their preoccupation with meeting the needs of the victims, they failed to ask: "Why do these children keep falling into the water somewhere upstream?"

In this book I have argued for restoring survivors of sexual abuse and those who have offended. I gave various examples to illustrate ways that encourage persons who have offended to face their harmful actions and to recognize the damage they have caused. A major goal of these methods is to prevent further offenses. However, if we talk about restoration for those who have offended without discussing the need to prevent the hurtful behaviors in the first place, we have completed only a portion of the task.

To return to the story about the children falling into the river, we should also ask, "Why is there a constant stream of persons who offend? What causes these many, many people to offend? How do we name and respond to the factors that contribute to their abusive patterns? How do we prevent the development of abusive behaviors?"

To answer these questions, we must take a fundamental and long-range view of relevant principles. I believe there are three major themes that provide a useful framework for beginning this process: *human sexuality, power dynamics,* and *theology.* I will address my comments primarily to the church community, the primary audience for this book.

Human Sexuality

We need to hear more proclamation from the pulpit about the gift of being created as sexual beings and in the image of God. Too often the church has focused on prohibiting sexual expression outside the context of a committed heterosexual relationship. But this is just one aspect of sexuality. As legitimate as that concern is, the church's preoccupation with it sends the message that sexuality in all its forms and expressions is somehow tainted.

When a subject has that strong a taboo, it is difficult to talk about the related questions and concerns. I am urging churches to develop openness to talking about sexuality, and preaching and learning about it. Thus we both can more fully appreciate this wonderful gift God has given us, and we are in a better position to prevent sexual abuse.

One challenging example comes from my work. Frequently, when I counsel a man who has offended, I discover that for him sexual orientation is an issue sometimes well hidden by denial and contrary belief. If such a person is a member of a faith community that does not accept homosexuality, he has a strong reason to drive underground urges that then may resurface in abusive ways.

This is not the place to lay out a particular response from the church community on homosexuality. However, I plead with the church to publicly acknowledge the reality of the individual's struggles with sexual orientation, so people could obtain suitable spiritual support. I also must state firmly that many heterosexuals sexually abuse children, and that many homosexuals never sexually harm a child.

Another example is the extensive use of pornography, especially by men. There are serious ethical and spiritual issues related to the flow of sexual images in magazines and more recently in videos and on the Internet. These images surround us every day and are not just of concern for a sermon once in a while.

Many Christians in their quest for pure Christian life and practice mostly ignore the existence of depersonalizing pornography. By their silence they seem to give approval to material that depicts people as objects for satisfying one's own lusts. I am always encouraged when I hear men who struggle with pornography tell me that they have found persons within their church community with whom they can be honest and open about these matters.

Power

I often wonder why it is so difficult for people to recognize and acknowledge that in many situations, some hold greater power than others. They often use that power to influence or control others. Perhaps because we tend to view power, like sexuality as a negative, we would rather pretend it does not exist.

From a prevention viewpoint, I must have an awareness of the power that I exert as a necessary step in avoiding its abuse. Those of us who are reluctant to recognize our power and the potential to use it in positive or negative ways may be exhibiting a false sense of humility and piety. This dangerous veneer must be shattered.

Theological Aspects

Theology provides a framework for applying biblical values and beliefs to daily life. Our basic understandings have a significant impact on how faith is lived on a daily basis. To expand our comprehension of human sexuality, power, forgiveness, and personal transformation, we need to develop our theology. We can do this by a more thorough study of the Bible and by learning from the social sciences and other disciplines.

By affirming masculinity and femininity as God-given gifts, we begin to affirm the wholesome goodness of sexuality. All persons are created in the image of God, and that is good.

Frequently Christians fear that a positive view of sexuality will promote sexual permissiveness. This fear unnecessarily clouds and confuses our message.

The Bible gives many examples of the use and abuse of power. Even if a church community believes in the equality of all persons, it can still accept the reality of differing roles in the exercise of power and authority. By recognizing the power we individually exercise in various church leadership roles, we put in place a process that allows us to more readily identify abuse of that entrusted power.

The gospel message of forgiveness has tremendous healing potential. Forgiveness needs to be linked with a process that includes accountability for wrongdoing and opportunities to rebuild trust. We must avoid any attempt to deal with the harm quickly and quietly. In this way, forgiveness provides a healing balm for many hurts in our society. I have witnessed its awesome effects on many wrongdoers and survivors of sexual abuse and their families.

Finally, we come to the heart of the gospel message. God's transforming power can produce miraculous, restorative change in the lives of men and women, survivors, sexual offenders, and all of us who seek and find God's healing touch.

Steps in Dealing with Sexual Abuse

The following list summarizes key steps we need to take to work wholistically and effectively with sexual abuse.

1. Sexual Abuse Hurts!

I have been profoundly affected by the people I have met who have been hurt by sexual abuse. It is intensely painful, emotionally and sometimes physically as well. Society's attitudes that minimize the trauma as "just touching" add more layers to the hurts. Sexual abusers also have hurts. They are part of a self-destructive cycle that has been carried on from generation to generation. Can we do our part to end the cycle of hurting?

2. Sexual Abuse Should Be Discussed Openly.

We cannot solve a problem if we do not acknowledge its existence. We must overcome our natural tendency to bury unsavory matters. In the past, we did not know about sexual abuse because we did not ask. We did not ask because we really did not want to know. Because of the conviction and courage of many people, that is changing. In the process, those affected by sexual abuse are being restored.

3. Sexual Wrongdoing Must Be Confronted Decisively and Compassionately.

To change the persistent patterns that underlie sexual wrongdoing, we must thoroughly and consistently address them over a period of time. Only then will new patterns be developed and followed. It is important to relate to wrongdoers with compassion. However, being compassionate does not mean we minimize the wrongful behavior or deal with it less conscientiously.

4. Restoration Is a Key Goal for Those Who Offend.

Restoration builds on three significant steps. First, people who have sexually offended must acknowledge their actions clearly and specifically. Second, they must develop an understanding of the deep and often irreparable harm experienced by the victim. Third, they need to demonstrate their changed behavior in their attitudes and their actions.

5. Offenders Must Come to Understand the Perspective of Victims.

Those who work with offenders insist that offenders develop a thorough awareness of the pain caused by sexual offending. The tension created by these two perspectives—victim and offender—are healthy ones that ensure a broader and more-helpful approach.

6. Sexual Abuse by Persons in Authority Has a Devastating Impact on More People.

Abuse by a church leader or other professional has an

intense ripple and wave effect far beyond the persons victimized. The impact on the larger group must be recognized and managed in a healing and supportive way.

7. It Is Crucial to Create Options for Healing.

Everyone who needs healing from a sexual affliction or hurt has had a unique experience. Those who have traveled the road before can point to signposts along the journey. At the same time, it is important to respect and encourage the integrity of people on their individual healing journeys.

8. Families and Churches Have a Role to Play in the Restoration of Those Who Offend.

Healing comes most effectively when we can connect with others in a mutual and supportive way. It cannot be a one-way street. Churches and families can offer reciprocal (two-way) relationships that increase the potential for healing and growth.

9. People Who Have Been Hurt Have Valuable Information to Share.

People in the Book Reference Group are examples of reciprocal relationships. Those who have experienced the pain of sexual abuse have shared with the broader community.

Thank you, Alexandra, Chip, Gary, Iris, Jimmy, Rebecca, Rob, Samantha, and Steve (see appendix 1). Your honest sharing will enrich the lives of many others.

Appendix
1

Personal Statements from the Book Reference Group

Alexandra

I am a woman and a survivor of sexual abuse. When this book was being created, I was in my late thirties and had been involved in counseling and therapy for about ten years. Healing from the turmoil and anguish that arose from my experience of abuse has been a major endeavor for me, and it will continue for the rest of my life. I chose to work on this book with Mark because contributing to the prevention of sexual abuse has great personal importance to me.

Through my involvement with Community Justice Initiatives, I have been involved in other workshops and discussions on the interplay between religion and sexual abuse. This particular focus intrigues me for both intellectual and personal reasons.

From an intellectual point of view, I believe that the patriarchal structures and doctrines (such as sacrifice, submission, baseness of body and sex) espoused by traditional North American religions play a role in allowing and perpetuating sexual abuse.

From a personal point of view, I feel that my family's religious beliefs opened the door for sexual abuse to occur and then prescribed "forgiveness" as the only way to heal myself from the ensuing trauma. I felt that religion had failed to protect me from abuse and had failed to provide me with support in my struggle to survive.

However, I am grateful that I have met individuals and communities who are examining religion's role in abusive situations, and who are committed to extracting the positive aspects religion offers. Religious communities must engage in critical self-examination and dedication to prevent sexual abuse and to provide a safe place for all those healing from its impact.

My participation in the Book Reference Group was both challenging and uplifting. One of the most important aspects was the opportunity to get to know and work beside men who had sexually offended in their pasts, men who are now committed to making a difference in their futures. This experience has played an important part in my healing journey. I am thankful to everyone who was there with me.

Chip

I am a student working toward a degree in counseling. For almost two years, I have been volunteering as a co-facilitator for men's support groups in a sexual offender program. I became interested in this topic by hearing a few men's stories and realizing that they are not hideous monsters without compassion or remorse. They are human beings who have made some mistakes in their lives, and they have problems just like everyone else.

As I began to work with these men, I started to see that they were not heartless or sex maniacs or perverts. Many of them have genuine sorrow for what they have done and carry that with them all the time. Many of them feel that they don't deserve to be treated with dignity or respect because of what they have done.

The men in the program at Community Justice Initiatives are different because they are willing to look at themselves with a critical eye. They are ready to accept what they need to work on. They are taking steps to get their lives back, to reclaim some of their dignity and self-worth—even to give back to others for the new lives that they have found.

I welcomed the opportunity to be involved in a group such as this because I believe that sexual abuse touches all of our lives, whether or not we have been victimized. I also believe that we all have a responsibility to do what we can to deal openly and honestly with the issue of sexual abuse in our homes, our churches, and in our communities. By reaching outside ourselves to establish loving relationships with others, we can help to heal the wounds that sexual abuse causes. We can help those who are victimized and those who have offended to reclaim their lives as they journey toward wholeness.

Gary

My name is Gary, and I am an ex-offender. I am forty-one years old and have been divorced since 1983. I am a professional musician and writer. I am also a self-diagnosed sex and love addict, which for me centers on fantasy-driven compulsive sexual activity. Since the age of twelve, I spent a good portion of my life engaged in fantasy and sexual acting out. As a result, I began attending a twelve-step group for sex and love addicts, similar to Alcoholics Anonymous, and recently celebrated my third anniversary.

I first became acquainted with Mark through the Sexual Abuse Treatment Program (SATP) at Community Justice Initiatives when I joined a group for offenders early in 1992. My process of recovery has not been without setbacks. At the end of 1992, I re-offended. This felt like betrayal—of myself, of the values I professed to hold, of my friends in the group, of those who placed their trust in me, my colleagues, my family, my friends, and most especially my victims. It really scared me and set me on a more determined path.

My second year in the group was more valuable. After leaving the group, I continued with the SATP as a part-time volunteer. My involvement with the book group came out of that. My reasons for wanting to be a part of this book are both simple and complex.

First, I am unabashedly grateful for the opportunity that Mark and SATP gave me to begin working on my redemption, and I wished to return the favor.

Second, belonging to the Book Reference Group was in fact part of my recovery process. I need to be able to talk freely about my offenses, how I let them take place, and what they meant. I need to be able, not to relive, but to revisit them because every time I do, there is the possibility of new awareness and understanding.

Third, the idea of bringing survivors and offenders together to contribute to a book about sexual abuse is unique. I think it was successful. Possibilities of this kind of interaction, education, prevention, and reconciliation need to be more fully explored. I can't begin to describe the range of emotions one goes through while listening to the stories and coming to realize that these are real people with real lives and real hurts, both survivors and offenders, and that many of the themes are similar to my own. Nor can I adequately express the admiration I feel for the courage of the group members in the face of shattered lives. For survivors, the term does not do them justice. They have accomplished far more than mere survival. The level of humor within our group is a sign that healing is possible.

Fourth, the book is important to me because it is education. As long as there are abusers, there will be survivors. The cycle has to stop, and armed with knowledge, we can begin to do that.

Finally, I am a writer. There aren't many settings in which I can speak so freely and safely about such a shame-filled but significant part of my life. Yet the writer's dictum is clear: Write what you know. I am an expert on the subject, as are all group members. They have lived it. I can only express my thanks to them and to Mark for letting me share what I know.

Iris

I am a survivor who chose to participate in the Book Reference Group because I wanted to understand the issues faced by those who have offended. I anticipated being able to learn and to share my insights. I was not disappointed. The group experience was quite positive, and I have gained new friends. Learning to relate to people who have offended is part of my healing journey.

I have been married thirty-one years; we have two adult sons. I am fifty-four years of age, and I began my healing journey eight years ago. When I began facing the issues of sexual abuse, my life fell apart: emotionally, sexually, spiritually, socially, and physically. Every facet of my life needed reconstruction. Our marriage suffered; it is a miracle from God that my husband and I now enjoy a happy, normal marriage. Sexual healing is being granted.

I am a Christian who dropped out of the church structure for three years, for purposes of healing. A complex set of triggers and flashbacks needed attention. I consider myself to have survived double incest—incest in the family and incest in the church. Coming back to church to take my rightful place has been challenging. I am back "in the fold" because people supported me, God heard my heart's desire, and I simply wouldn't give up on finding my way back.

I struggled with questions of how to relate to God and to people in a trusting way. I rebelled against the love of God, submission, being used of God, losing my life, and offering my body as a living sacrifice. Why couldn't I forgive once and for all? I began to shed a lifelong habit of getting out of messes all by myself. (I had come to believe that I had gotten into this mess all by myself!). Instead, I learned to "let God." God's way is far superior, the only way truly to be free.

I stripped my spiritual life of all pious or spiritual words in an effort to find what was real, true, and basic. Jesus was the only stable one in all this dissecting and reconstruction. I owe my life to Jesus and the power of his resurrection. The love of God made this incredible journey possible. Spiritual healing is being granted.

Jimmy

When I was asked if I would like to help with the book that Mark was writing, at first I didn't jump at the chance. I thought, as I always do, "What can I contribute?"

I was asked a few more times, and then I made up my mind to help, because by then I realized that this book would be different, and that this book could help a lot of people. It also would give me a chance to give something back.

At the first meeting, I saw that the rest of the group was made up of about four male offenders and an equal number of female survivors. I thought to myself again that this book was worth doing. Everything in it was coming "from the horse's mouth," so to speak.

As an ex-offender, I had an opportunity to work alongside female survivors and get to know them, and to learn how they are feeling and all about their hurt. Every time we got together, we had some emotional times and a lot of laughter.

I would like to think that I made some new friends. I do believe that participating in a group at Community Justice Initiatives allows for growth, and I think that is why ex-offenders and female survivors can become friends.

I am thankful that some people can reach deep into their hearts and find forgiveness. Otherwise, offenders may never find the courage to turn their lives around.

So to all of you who know how to forgive, a warm and heartfelt THANK YOU. Without you, who knows where a lot of offenders might be today. A little love and understanding can make a difference. We who were offenders have turned our lives around because of people just like you. From the bottom of my heart, thanks! I will always remember those who reached out a helping hand.

Rebecca

I am a female survivor of childhood sexual abuse, in my mid-thirties. I began to work on sexual abuse issues about five years ago. I feel that I have made much progress. The longer I work on these issues, the more I realize that in some form or another, the abuse that I suffered as a child has always been a major factor in my life and will continue to be so.

It has been rewarding and challenging for me to begin to

reach out and help others who are walking paths similar to mine. To that end I have done much writing and public speaking, and I have cooperated in leading survivor support groups. I strongly believe that sexual abuse is something that can and needs to be voiced, out loud, honestly, and with no loss of face.

Being a part of Mark's book group was born out of telling my story to groups of persons who had sexually offended. I had expected to feel angry and upset, and was surprised when I left those meetings feeling quite hopeful, even powerful. I saw how helpful it is for there to be honest though painful communication between survivors and offenders in a *safe* setting.

I watched with cynical eyes as men who had molested children broke down and cried when they heard my story. Afterward they asked me for reassurance that their victims would be okay, reassurance that I could not give.

I saw the new group members' walls of denial being attacked head-on—no holds barred—not by group leaders but by longtime group members. Such effective confrontation came from those in Mark's book group who have taken responsibility for what they have done. I realized that while I had no words of comfort to give these people, I did have a new respect for persons trying to come to terms with the terrible things they had done, and at the same time trying to heal themselves to prevent re-offending. I learned that honesty and holding people accountable for their actions does not have to include disdain.

I count it a privilege to be part of this book. I had expected to be challenged by being a part of a group that included both survivors and persons who had sexually offended—and a challenge it certainly was! I did not expect the friendships and even love that developed. At no time did I disarm my internal lie detector apparatus. I didn't stop being angry at what was done to me. I remain cynical about forgiveness and the way it is often used to silence victims. I simply learned that when people take responsibility for what they have done, they can make real changes, and trust can be revived.

Rob

It has been a privilege for me to have a small part in putting this book together. As one who offended, this project was a part of my healing. I came into the group to help; however, mostly I found myself being helped.

During the period when I was able to attend the Book Reference Group sessions, I was able to bring out personal issues that I still needed to face. For both survivors and offenders, abuse seems to stay with us for a long time, even a lifetime. Pain and hurtful memories are always with us, and we need help to overcome.

I strongly believe that the church with God's grace is able to help survivors and offenders deal with personal issues, to help their personal growth, and to help the healing process so each survivor and offender can receive maximum healing.

The church is the tool God has chosen to reach hurting people in a lost world. My prayer is that this book can be a tool to reach these hurting people.

Samantha

My name is Samantha, Sam for short. Actually, that is not my real name, but I wanted to pick one that could work for a boy or a girl, because that is how I managed to stay relatively unharmed. My mother (while unable to protect me in so many other ways) made sure of one thing: I was to stay unattractive to the gaze of male predators—transformed from a girl to a boy. My hair was cut very short, and I was dressed mainly in jeans. I climbed trees more fearlessly than any boy in the neighborhood, to great applause, and I moved awkwardly when wearing a pretty dress.

When finally my body started to go through its natural changes and the girlishness could no longer be denied, I found that intellect if used well could have the same outcome. I was barely twelve years young when I was able to intimidate with words. Such intimidation meant hiding my vulnerability, that vulnerability so often associated for all of us with femininity.

I am thirty-six now, have been relatively successful in my

career, and am a mother of one. I am only now beginning to trust that being a woman might be okay. You see, I am a cosurvivor of sexual abuse. Don't get me wrong—things happened to me too. When I was only ten, I saw two exhibitionists on my way to school. A doctor fumbled me when I was thirteen and in pain, needing his help. A boy in the neighborhood tried to insert objects into me (just as had been done to him?). Later, much later, I was raped by a man I lived with. Believe it or not, that is not where my pain lies—not yet.

When I was three, I went to live for two years with my grandparents, who were devoted Roman Catholics: holy water at every corner of the house, a firm place for men and women in the world, a sense that pain had to be endured for the grace of God. In their bedroom (where I also slept), they had a statue of Jesus gently placing his finger on his lips, reminding all good Christians to be silent. Silent, so I figured out, about those things adults do with each other or adults do with children.

So . . . I saw much but said nothing! I would not even dare to tell my imaginary friend, who provided comfort in so many ways when I felt troubled. We were silent about so many things, and it was hard to keep up with all the boundaries and secrets, trying not to mix up whom you tell what.

So how in all this silence I knew that my father was assaulted by a priest when he was very young, I don't remember. Anyhow, it is because of that abuse, so the stories go, that he was always having nervous breakdowns, having to go to psychiatric hospitals, or described as a "coward," "weak," and "stuck in the past." I have not seen my father in many years, but I always felt sorry for him—even when he would use me to cry on, shaking like a child, needing my secrecy about that "weakness."

After he had left, never to be part of my life again, my sister was born. She in turn was abused by a blind priest whom my mother had befriended. I knew, and this time I spoke out—but not loudly enough. Why would a man of God, a person sought by many for spiritual advice and stricken by a sudden disability, do any such thing? We must have misunderstood. . . . So the abuse continued. He died, leaving two young women years later sitting in a pub guiltily admitting relief about his death. To this day his image in the community is untainted.

I drifted into work, trying to understand why people hurt people sexually, and learning that in turn they often had been hurt too. But more to the point—the circle closes—silence had prevented them from sharing that pain. Secrecy does not make things go away. It just hides them—until they come back to haunt us in other ways. I don't go to church anymore, but I would like to move that finger away from Jesus' mouth. In my "religion," it doesn't belong there. You see, I believe that until we speak, we are all cosurvivors of abuse. When one of us hurts and we say nothing, we all end up hurting.

I joined the Book Reference Group because talking about these things is so important, because silence does a disservice to all the three-year-old little girls who know so much and say so little. When the answer to a question is so hard to find, we just might find it in each other. I admire Mark for having the courage to organize the group. I admire and respect my fellow group members for being there and for telling their stories. I thank them for being *model speakers* who have helped me to begin to speak some of my truths. I hope the readers appreciate that opportunity as much as I did. Silence is anathema!

Steve

My name is Steve. When I was asked to be a part of this book-writing project, I was excited. For me, it was another step in my journey toward healing. I came to this project as a person who has offended sexually. As a result of this behavior, I was incarcerated for thirteen months. I lost my job and my family.

During my time in prison, I gradually became aware of the amount of inner pain I carried as well as the devastating pain I inflicted upon my victim-survivor and my family.

Upon my release, I continued to receive counseling through male offender groups. I am now a volunteer with Community Justice Initiatives.

While in prison, I received a tremendous amount of support from family, friends, and my church community, through telephone, visits, cards, and letters. My victim, not as fortunate, received little support and was blamed for what happened. As I received all this support, I wondered how much the church really understood about sexual abuse, how to deal with offenders, and how to support survivors.

I hope that by sharing our stories and thoughts in this group setting, we will be able to help churches understand and to give them tools in their dealings with sexual abuse.

Appendix

2

Sample Forms

Peer Review Outline[1]

1. Name _____
2. Age _____
3. What were the offenses and/or charges?

Please consider and answer these questions:

The Offense

1. How did the sexual abuse happen?
2. How did your position of power help you to offend?
3. What types of situations are high risk for you? How do you handle them?

You

1. Describe how you meet your needs for comfort, love, and nurture.
2. How do you know when your boundaries have been crossed? When others' boundaries have been crossed?
3. What is healing for you? For your victim(s)? For your relationship with your community?

Being a Parent, Caregiver, or Adult

1. Describe your position of authority and how you misused it.

2. How important is trust to a child, and how do you think a child is affected by a betrayal of trust?

3. Describe healthy communication patterns, and identify how you work to improve your communication patterns.

Your Relationship with Your Partner and Family

1. What helps you to identify and talk about both positive and negative feelings in your partner relationship?

2. Which ways of thinking and/or behaving have helped you to identify your sexual needs and issues? How do you know when you are ignoring your sexual needs and issues?

3. What has been your past sexual abuse cycle, and how do you acknowledge the risk of slipping back into that cycle?

Your Level of Participation in the Group

1. What does it mean to take a risk in group? Describe your *feelings* about taking risks.

2. Give examples of you giving and receiving feedback, and your involvement in confrontation.

3. Which of your behaviors demonstrates your commitment to change?

Invitation to Facilitated Family Dialogue

This sample letter was prepared by an abuse victim who invited his nine siblings (including his older brother who had been the abuser) and two parents to come to a family conference. They all attended. They talked openly and developed family guidelines to increase the level of safety for family members who had children. They planned follow-up to ensure that treatment issues had been fully addressed.

The Invitation Letter

Dear _____:

I would like to invite you to a family conference on Friday, February 21, 1996, at 2:00 p.m. at 241 Weber St. E., Kitchener, Ontario.

The purpose of this conference is to provide an opportunity for honest and open discussion about sexual abuse as it was experienced in our family. This discussion will be strictly confidential. A consent form for facilitated dialogue is enclosed and must be signed by all family members.

Along with immediate family members, Mark Yantzi and Lynda ____ from Community Justice Initiatives will be present to facilitate this mediation. This process is an alternative to the criminal justice system.

If you have any questions or concerns about this conference, Mark and Lynda will respond to your telephone calls or arrange a visit. You can call them at ____.

Your presence would be greatly appreciated. If you have any concerns about the date or time chosen, please call me at ____.

The cost of this conference and facilitated dialogue will be covered by a donation to the agency from us, the participants.

Your brother and son,

____

Tricks, Traps, Lures in Sexually Offending

A member of the Book Reference Group has compiled the following list of strategies used to offend against children. These abusive incidents are not random and accidental happenings, as offenders may pretend.

Jimmy's list demonstrates numerous approaches used to achieve a goal and in the process disempower and blame the child victim.

He acknowledges that he himself has used some of these tricks. He heard of other lures in various groups or in one-to-one discussions over several years.

Jimmy makes presentations to community groups, to groups of offenders, and groups of survivors. Survivors often respond to his presentation with relief and understanding. They realize that a child really is not equipped to effectively reject these approaches by a self-serving adult.

Here is the list compiled by Jimmy:

Strategies

Making Threats

Break up the family
Hurt the child
Loss of privileges
Child will get in trouble
Family will have to move
Never see your friends again

Taking Total Control

Domineering
Use of anger
Silent treatment
Building trust
Arranging time alone with child
Bribes or promises
Invading child's privacy
Favoring the child over others
More lenient in disciplining the child
Taking the child places to ingratiate and obligate him/her

Imposing Guilt Trips

Telling the child, "You like" the sexualized activity
Saying nobody will believe the child
Saying it is preparation for sex in the future
Telling the child, "You asked for it in your sleep"
Using the word "we" as if both are part of it
Saying to child, "Don't you love me?"

Letting the Child Feel in Control

Stopping when the child says "no"
Giving the child the illusion of choice
"Asking" child for "permission"

Community Reintegration Project

This pilot project of the Mennonite Central Committee Ontario seeks to reduce the risk of re-offense by released sex offenders, to ease their transition into the community, and to open an avenue for victims in their journey for restoration and healing.[1]

The project seeks to prevent further victimization both through reducing relapse by offenders and by increasing public awareness of the roots of sexual violence and abuse. The project also seeks to enhance the safety of the community, the victims(s), and the ex-offender.

The community. The risk for the community lies in the first offense and then in the possibility of re-offense. Our first concern is to minimize any risk to children. Sexual offenses against children are among the most abhorrent because they are so defenseless. Abuse of adults is also horrible, and it affects children and the whole community.

The victim(s). Our concern is to bring needed healing to all victims, protect them in their vulnerability, and deal with fears that the offender will violate the same victims again or someone close to them.

The ex-offender. Our concern is to hold him accountable to the terms of his voluntary covenant for responsible behavior, to protect his rights as a citizen, and to help him cope with the reaction of the community, police, and media.

Circle of Support and Accountabllity

A Covenant Relationship

The project involves volunteers from the faith community forming a Circle of Support and Accountability to help facilitate the reintegration of offenders released from prison and legal supervision.

The circle and the ex-offender agree on a covenant that includes a commitment by the ex-offender to accept the circle's help and advice, to pursue a predetermined course of treatment, and to act responsibly in the community.

The circle helps provide a healthy environment for the ex-offender. It also fulfills roles such as these:

Advocating with various systems. The circle works in cooperation with the police, neighborhood groups, victims, and treatment professionals.

Confronting the ex-offender when necessary about his attitudes and behavior.

Walking with him through emergencies.

Mediating community concerns.

Celebrating anniversaries, milestones, and all the small victories in his journey to reintegration.

Guiding Principles of the Circle

We affirm that the community bears a responsibility for the reintegration of offenders and the restoration of victims.

We believe in a loving and reconciling God, who calls us to be agents of healing work in this world.

We acknowledge the ongoing pain of victims of sexual abuse and their need for healing.

We welcome the offender into the community and into accountability. When community does not exist for them, we seek to re-create community with them in responsible, safe, healthy, and life-giving ways.

We accept God's call to radical hospitality, sharing our lives with one another in community and taking risks in the service of love.

Notes

Preface
1. See description in chapter 4.

1. Beginning to Talk
1. D. Finkelhor and D. Russell, "Women as Perpetrators," in *Child Sexual Abuse*, ed. D. Finkelhor (New York: Free Press, 1984), 171-185.

2. C. Allen, "Women as Perpetrators of Child Sexual Abuse: Recognition Barriers," in *The Incest Offender: The Family Member No One Wants to Treat*, ed. A. Horton, B. Johnson, L. Roundy, and D. Williams (Newbury Park, Calif.: Sage, 1990), 109-125; L. Robinson, N. Coady, and L.Tutty, "Females Who Sexually Abuse Children," in *Qualitative Research for Social Workers: Phases, Steps, Tasks*, ed. L. Tutty, M. Rothery, and R. Grinnell (Boston, Mass.: Allyn and Bacon, 1996), 152-173.

3. Committee on Restorative Justice, 1981.

4. Rates of re-offending vary greatly with various sexual offenses, the offender's background, and available appropriate treatment. On this question, see chapter 10, "The Case for Treatment," in W. L. Marshall and Sylvia Barrett, *Criminal Neglect: Why Sex Offenders Go Free* (Toronto: Doubleday Canada, 1990).

2. The Hurts of Sexual Abuse
1. Viktor E. Frankl, *Man's Search for Meaning* (Boston: Beacon Press, 1985), 64. For personal statements by Rebecca and others in the Book Reference Group, see appendix 1.

2. Ellen Bass and Laura Davis, *The Courage to Heal: A Guide for Women Survivors of Child Sexual Abuse* (New York: Harper & Row, 1988), 22.

3. C. Badgely and W. Thurston, "Juvenile Prostitution and Child Sexual Abuse: A Controlled Study," *Canadian Journal of Community Mental Health* 6:5-26.

3. Why Sexual Abuse Takes Place

1. See personal statements by members of the Book Reference Group in appendix 1.

2. Alan Jenkins, *Invitation to Responsibility: The Therapeutic Engagement of Men Who Are Violent and Abusive* (Adelaide, Australia: Dulwich Centre Pubns., 1990), appendix V: "Restraints to Men Taking Responsibility for Abuse."

3. The speaker was Carolyn Holderread Heggen, at Breslau, Ontario, spring of 1994.

4. A man who had offended tried to keep his daughter from reporting him by telling her that the harsh punishment of the courts would hurt the family.

5. R. Mathews, J. Mathews, and K. Speltz, "Female Sex Offenders," in *The Sexually Abused Male*, ed. M. Hunter (Lexington, Mass.: Heath, 1990), 1:275-293.

6. On this issue and the detrimental impact it can have on clients and their families, see Michael Yapko, "The Seductions of Memory," *The Family Therapy Networker*, Sept.-Oct. 1993, 31-37.

7. For a discussion of various viewpoints on the issue of memory and the repressed memory controversy, see *American Psychologist*, May 1994, 439-444.

4. Restorative Justice

1. On new models and paradigms, see Howard Zehr, *Changing Lenses: A New Focus for Crime and Justice* (Scottdale, Pa.: Herald Press, 1990).

2. Adapted from a 1981 statement by the Committee on Restorative Justice, supported by: Community Justice Initiatives, Quaker Committee on Jails and Justice, Mennonite Central Committee, Rittenhouse-New Vision, and Conflict Mediation Services. Copy available from MCC Ontario, 50 Kent Ave., Kitchener, ON N2G 3R1, Canada.

3. For an outline, see "Tricks, Traps, Lures," in appendix 2.

4. For a fuller discussion of restorative justice and sexual abuse, see the unpublished article by Heather Block and Chris Lichti, "Restorative Justice with Respect to Domestic Violence and Sexual Abuse." Available from Voices for Nonviolence, 134 Plaza Drive, Winnipeg, MB R3T 5K9, Canada.

5. Applying Restorative Justice

1. See unpublished article above, in note 4 to chapter 4.

2. For a framework, see peer review outline in appendix 2.

3. For more information on roles and issues for mothers, see Tracy Orr, *No Right Way* (Chicago: Login Pubs. Consortium InBook, 1995).

4. See "When the Abuser Is Among Us: One Church's Response to a Perpetrator," *Working Together to Prevent Sexual and Domestic Violence* 14 (no. 3, winter 1993-spring 1994), Seattle: Center for the Prevention of Sexual and Domestic Violence.

6. Abuse by a Church Leader

1. Private correspondent, no. 1, adapted.

2. Patrick Carnes, *Out of the Shadows*, 2d ed., ed. Jane T. Noland (Center City, Minn.: Hazeldon Educational Materials, 1992), says not all sexual addicts are offenders or vice versa. His book provides a helpful overview and clearly portrays how far some go to satisfy their sexually addictive desires.

3. Marie M. Fortune, "Informal Mediated Processes in Response to Complaints of Clergy Misconduct," *Occasional Papers*, no. 2 (Seattle: Center for the Prevention of Sexual and Domestic Violence, Jan. 1995).

4. Private correspondent, no. 2.

5. Private correspondent, no. 2.

6. Wilson, Earl and Sandy, Paul and Virginia Friesen, Larry and Paul Paulson, *Restoring the Fallen: A Team Approach to Caring, Confronting, and Reconciling* (Downers Grove, Ill.: InterVarsity Press, 1997).

7. How Does Healing Come?

1. Source unknown; from bulletin board at Community Justice Initiatives and shared with many people dealing with past sexual abuse.

2. See Jenkins, *Invitation to Responsibility*, for a more detailed consideration of how to assist persons who have offended to take responsibility for their own past behaviors.

3. Private correspondent, no. 3.

8. Unresolved Hurts from Abuse

1. For additional background, see Vern Redekopp, "Scapegoats, the Bible, and Criminal Justice: Interacting with René Girard," *Occasional Papers*, no. 13 (Akron, Pa.: MCC Office of Criminal Justice, Feb. 1993).

2. See Peter Rutter, *Sex in the Forbidden Zone: When Men in Power—Therapists, Doctors, Clergy, Teachers, and Others—Betray Women's Trust* (New York: Jeremy P. Tarcher, Putnam Publishing Group, 1989).

3. Statistics on the frequency of sexual abuse vary depending on how the sexual abuse is defined and the scope of the study. For a discussion of this issue, see C. Bagley and K. King, *Child Sexual Abuse: The Search for Healing* (New York: Tavistock, Routledge, 1989), chapter 4, "Statistical Dimensions."

9. What About Forgiveness?

1. Private correspondent, no. 4.
2. Private correspondent, no. 5.
3. Frederick Keene, "The Politics of Forgiveness," *Working Together to Prevent Sexual and Domestic* 16 (no. 1, fall 1995), Seattle: Center for the Prevention of Sexual and Domestic Violence.
4. Private correspondent, no. 5.

10. A Caring Church Responding

1. As explained here, support-accountability groups are different from accountability groups sometimes set up by church disciplinary bodies for a probationary period to monitor and supervise a congregational leader who has been sexually abusive.
2. For more on the church's supportive role, see Joanne Ross Feldmeth and Midge Wallace Finley, *We Weep for Ourselves and Our Children: A Christian Guide for Survivors of Childhood Sexual Abuse* (San Francisco: Harper San Francisco, 1990).

11. Facilitated Dialogue

1. Private correspondent, no. 5.
2. In outlining this model, I used a paper by Tammie Brunk: "An Alternative to the Criminal Justice System: Mediation Services for People Healing from Sexual Abuse," prepared for Community Justice Initiatives, Apr. 1994. In this chapter the term "facilitated dialogue" avoids confusion with some aspects of mediation that imply mutual responsibility for aspects of the offending act(s).
3. See sample invitation letter in appendix 2.
4. Private correspondent, no. 5.
5. For more on this issue, see Fortune, "Informal Mediated Processes in Response to Complaints of Clergy Misconduct."

12. Restorative Justice in Difficult Cases

1. For more on sexual addiction, see Carnes, *Out of the Shadows.*
2. For a description of one model which seeks to reintegrate repeat sexual offenders, see description in appendix 3.
3. As defined in 1981 by the Committee on Restorative Justice, supported by: Community Justice Initiatives, Quaker Committee on Jails and Justice, Mennonite Central Committee, Rittenhouse-New Vision, and Conflict Mediation Services.

13. Restorative Justice Working

1. Her name and others in this account have been changed.
2. See appendix 3 for a description of the Community Integration

Project, utilizing Circles of Support to assist in the reintegration of released sex offenders.

3. The term "dual relationships" refers to individuals being interconnected in several ways, with more than one form of relationship, such as both also attending the same church. That is not necessarily a problem if both parties agree to it. In this instance, Lorraine wanted to avoid complications and have a relationship with only one dimension: a survivor and one who had offended, discussing their journeys.

4. After participating in the weekend workshop in 1995, Melissa A. Miller wrote this description. She is the author of *Family Violence: The Compassionate Church Responds* (Scottdale, Pa.: Herald Press, 1994).

Appendix 2: Sample Forms

1. This Peer Review Outline as developed is used in the Sexual Abuse Treatment Program of Community Justice Initiatives.

Appendix 3: Community Reintegration

1. For more information on this initiative, please contact Mennonite Central Committee Ontario, 50 Kent Ave., Kitchener, ON N2G 3R1, Canada. Funding received from Correctional Services Canada.

Bibliography

America Friends Service Committee. *Struggle for Justice: A Report on Crime and Justice in America*. New York: Hill & Wang, 1971.

Bagley, Christopher, and Kathleen King. *Child Sexual Abuse: The Search for Healing*. New York: Tavistock, Routledge, 1989.

Bass, Ellen, and Laura Davis. *The Courage to Heal: A Guide for Women Survivors of Child Sexual Abuse*. New York: Harper & Row, 1988.

Bays, Laren, and Robert Freeman-Longo. *Who Am I and Why Am I in Treatment?* Brandon, Vt.: Safer Society, 1988.

_____. *Why Did I Do It Again? Understanding My Cycle of Problem Behavior*. Brandon, Vt.: Safer Society, 1989.

Bays, Laren, Robert Freeman-Longo, and Diane D. Hildebran. *How Can I Stop? Breaking My Abuse Cycle*. Brandon, Vt.: Safer Society, 1990.

Bear, Euan, with Peter Dimock. *Adults Molested as Children: A Survivor's Manual for Men and Women*. Brandon, Vt.: Safer Society, 1990.

Block, Isaac. *Assault on God's Image: Domestic Abuse*. Winnipeg: Windflower Communications, 1991.

Boers, Arthur Paul. *Justice That Heals: A Biblical Vision for Victims and Offenders*. Newton, Kan.: Faith & Life Press, 1992.

Carnes, Patrick. *Out of the Shadows*. 2d ed. Ed. Jane T. Noland. Center City, Minn.: Hazeldon Educational Materials, 1992.

Corrigan, William T. *"Journeys of Darkness, Journeys of Light: Male Sexual Offenders' Perceptions of Spirituality."* Unpublished comprehensive paper. Waterloo, Ont.: Waterloo Lutheran Seminary, 1996.

Feldmeth, Joanne Ross, and Midge Wallace Finley. *We Weep for Ourselves and Our Children: A Christian Guide for Survivors of Sexual Abuse*. San Francisco: Harper San Francisco, 1990.

Finkelhor, David. *A Sourcebook on Child Sexual Abuse*. Newbury Park, Calif.: Sage Pubns., 1986.

Fortune, Marie M. *Sexual Violence: The Unmentionable Sin.* New York: Pilgrim Press, 1989.

_____. *Is Nothing Sacred? When Sex Invades the Pastoral Relationship.* San Francisco: HarperCollins, 1989.

_____. "Informal Mediated Processes in Response to Complaints of Clergy Misconduct." In *Occasional Papers*, no. 2. Seattle: Center for the Prevention of Sexual and Domestic Violence, Jan. 1995.

Funk, Rus Ervin. *Stopping Rape: A Challenge for Men.* Philadelphia: New Society Pubs., 1993.

Giaretto, H. *Integrated Treatment of Child Sexual Abuse: A Treatment and Training Model.* Palo Alto, Calif.: Science & Behavior Books, 1982.

Grubman, Stephen D. *Broken Boys, Mending Men: Recovery from Childhood Sexual Abuse.* Blue Ridge Summit, Pa.: TAB Books, 1990.

Hancock, Maxine, and Karen Burton Mains. *Child Sexual Abuse: A Hope for Healing.* Wheaton, Ill.: Harold Shaw, 1988.

Hargrave, Terry. *Families and Forgiveness: Healing Wounds in the Intergenerational Family.* New York: Bruner/Mazel, 1994.

Heggen, Carolyn Holderread. *Sexual Abuse in Christian Homes and Churches.* Scottdale, Pa.: Herald Press, 1993.

Hopkins, Nancy Myer, and Mark Laaser, eds. *Restoring the Soul of the Church: Healing Congregations Wounded by Clergy Sexual Misconduct.* Collegeville, Minn.: The Alban Institute, 1995.

Horton, A., B. Johnson, L. Roundy, and D. Williams. *The Incest Offender: The Family Member No One Wants to Treat.* Newbury Park, Calif.: Sage Pubns., 1990.

Jenkins, Alan. *Invitation to Responsibility: The Therapeutic Engagement of Men Who Are Violent and Abusive.* Adelaide, Australia: Dulwich Centre Pubns., 1990.

Knopf, Fay Honey. *Retraining Adult Sex Offenders: Methods and Models.* Branden, Vt.: Safer Society, 1984.

Lee, John H. *The Flying Boy.* Deerfield Beacon, Fla.: Health Communications, 1987.

Lew, Michael. *Victims No Longer: Men Recovering from Incest.* New York: Harper & Row, 1988.

MacCullam-Paterson, Morton. *Toward a Justice That Heals.* Toronto: United Church Publishing House, 1988.

Marshall, W. L., and Sylvia Barrett. *Criminal Neglect: Why Sex Offenders Go Free.* Toronto: Doubleday Canada, 1990.

Mathews, R., J. Matthews, and K. Speltz. *Female Sex Offender: An Exploratory Study.* Branden, Vt.: Safer Society, 1989.

Mayer, Adele. *Sex Offenders: Approaches to Understanding and Management.* Holmes Beach, Fla.: Learning Pubns., 1988.

Miller, Dee Ann. *How Little We Knew: Collusion and Confusion with Sexual Misconduct.* Lafayette, La.: Prescott Press, 1993.

Miller, Melissa, A. *Family Violence: The Compassionate Church Responds.* Scottdale, Pa.: Herald Press, 1994.

Northey, Wayne. "Restorative Justice: Rebirth of an Ancient Practice." *Occasional Papers,* no. 14. Akron, Pa.: MCC Office of Criminal Justice, Feb. 1994.

Poling, James N. *The Abuse of Power: A Theological Problem.* Nashville: Abingdon, 1991.

Prendergast, William E. *Treating Sex Offenders in Correctional Institutions and Outpatient Clinics: A Guide to Clinical Practice.* New York: Haworth Press, 1991.

Pryor, Douglas P. *Unspeakable Acts: Why Men Sexually Abuse Children.* New York: New York Univ. Press, 1996.

Redekopp, Vern. "Scapegoats, the Bible, and Criminal Justice: Interacting with René Girard." *Occasional Papers,* no. 13. Akron, Pa.: MCC Office of Criminal Justice, Feb. 1993.

Ridings, K. C. *Facing the Brokenness.* Scottdale, Pa.: Herald Press, 1991.

Ross, Ruppert. *Returning to the Teachings: Exploring Aboriginal Justice.* Toronto: Penguin Books, 1996.

Sadelar, Christiane. "An Ounce of Prevention: The Life Stories and Perceptions of Men Who Sexually Offended Against Children." Master's thesis. Waterloo, Ont.: Wilfrid Laurier Univ., Dept. of Psychology, 1994.

Salter, Anna C. *Treating Child Sex Offenders and Victims.* Newbury Park, Calif.: Sage Pubns., 1988.

____. *Transforming Trauma.* Newbury Park, Calif.: Sage Pubns., 1995.

Schlesinger, Benjamin, ed. *Sexual Abuse of Children in the 1980s.* Toronto: Univ. of Toronto Press, 1986.

Wilson, Earl and Sandy, Paul and Virginia Friesen, Larry and Paul Paulson. *Restoring the Fallen: A Team Approach to Caring, Confronting, and Reconciling.* Downers Grove, Ill.: InterVarsity Press, 1997.

Wodarski, John S., and Daniel Whitaker, eds. *The Treatment of Sex Offenders in Social Work and Mental Health Settings.* New York: Haworth Press, 1989.

Wright, Martin, and Burt Galaway, eds. *Mediation and Criminal Justice: Victims, Offenders, and Community.* Newbury Park, Calif.: Sage Pubns., 1989.

Zehr, Howard. *Changing Lenses: A New Focus for Crime and Justice.* Scottdale, Pa.: Herald Press, 1990.

The Author

Mark Yantzi has been a coordinator with the Sexual Abuse Treatment Program of Community Justice Initiatives, Kitchener-Waterloo, since 1982. In 1976 he was involved in the initiation of the first Victim Offender Reconciliation Program (VORP) in North America. From 1970 to 1981, he was a probation and parole officer with the Ministry of Correctional Services for the Province of Ontario.

Yantzi earned a bachelor's degree in sociology at the University of Waterloo in Ontario. During the second year of that program, he studied at International Christian University in Tokyo. In 1976 he received a master of applied science degree in human relations and counseling from the University of Waterloo. Some requirements for this program were met through courses taken at Mennonite Biblical Seminary, Elkhart, Indiana.

He is a clinical member of the American Association for Marriage and Family Therapy and has completed specialized training in sexual therapy, divorce mediation, and sexual misconduct by professionals. In various settings in Canada, United States, and England, Yantzi has presented many workshops dealing with criminal justice alternatives, community responses to sexual abuse, and responding to sexual offending.

Since 1982 Yantzi has been an elected member of Kitchener (Ontario) City Council; he has represented the city on the Region of Waterloo Council since 1984. As a councillor, he worked for the development of nonprofit housing and promoted neighborhood involvement and urban core redevelopment.

Mark Yantzi was born in Ontario and lives in Kitchener with his wife, Glennis, a community-based mental health nurse. They have two sons, Michael and Jamie. The family attends a house church that is in a cluster of ecumenical house-church groups affiliated with the Mennonite Church.

Related Books from Herald Press

Family Violence: The Compassionate Church Responds
Melissa A Miller

Pregnant and Single
Carolyn Owens and Linda Roggow

Sexual Abuse in Christian Homes and Churches
Carolyn Holderread Heggen

Beyond the News . . . Sexual Abuse
Mennonite Media Ministries Video
Featuring Carolyn Holderread Heggen
With stories by survivors of sexual abuse
An aid in the study of Heggen's book

Sexual Offending and Restoration
Mark Yantzi

Women and Men: Gender in the Church
Edited by Carol Penner

Toll-free ordering:
1-800-759-4447